The Unconventional Career of Dr Muriel Bell

'Karaka, *Corynocarpus laevigatus*, leaves and berries', from
An Encyclopaedia of New Zealand, 1966, ed. A.H. McLintock.
Te Ara – the Encyclopedia of New Zealand

The Unconventional Career of Dr Muriel Bell

DIANA BROWN

OTAGO

Published by Otago University Press
Level 1, 398 Cumberland Street
Dunedin, New Zealand
university.press@otago.ac.nz
www.otago.ac.nz/press

First published 2018

ISBN 978-1-98-853130-4

A catalogue record for this book is available from the National Library of New Zealand.

Editor: Erika Bűky
Index: Diane Lowther
Design/layout: Fiona Moffat

Cover: Muriel Bell, 1940. *New Zealand Free Lance: Photographic prints and negatives, Ref: PAColl-6388-52, Alexander Turnbull Library, Wellington*

Printed in Christchurch by Caxton

CONTENTS

Introduction

A LIFE IN NUTRITION RESEARCH

Dr Muriel Bell (1898–1974) contributed widely to the field of nutritional science throughout her career. One of the few New Zealand women of her era to obtain the research degree of medical doctor, she studied physiology and the emerging field of biochemistry, focusing on the connections between disease and nutritional deficiencies. She was appointed New Zealand's first state nutritionist in 1940 and retained that position until her retirement in 1964.

Muriel Bell helped to establish nutrition and dietetics as professional fields in New Zealand. In her early research fieldwork, her capacity for what might now be called lateral thinking helped to identify deficiencies in soil minerals that were causing a mysterious illness in livestock. Experts in Britain, where she studied for several years in leading teaching hospitals and research institutions, identified Muriel as 'an exceptional woman with the very rare instinct of the true researcher'.[1]

As a public official, she increased scientific and popular knowledge of nutrition and radically improved the standard of nutrition in New Zealand by instituting the distribution of milk in schools; promoting the iodisation of table salt to prevent thyroid disease; campaigning vigorously in favour of public water fluoridation to combat tooth decay; and disseminating advice on healthy eating through radio talks, numerous magazine articles and nutritional handbooks like *Good Nutrition*. Her research on vitamins and minerals helped prevent deficiency diseases, especially in children, and her work on dietary fats and cholesterol helped to shed light on the growing problem of coronary heart disease. Her research and public service took her to Vienna, Britain, the Pacific Islands, Asia and the United States.

This work was carried out against a backdrop of dramatic historical events and scientific advances. In New Zealand and around the globe, the years spanning the two world wars exposed a wide range of health problems in the general population and gave birth to the modern understanding of public health. The Depression and years of wartime and postwar austerity had led to poverty and malnutrition. With advances in the scientific understanding of nutrition, including the roles of vitamins, minerals and other micronutrients in the body, scientists could identify specific causes for many conditions previously thought of simply as diseases of poverty, and propose remedies. Addressing such problems required cooperation and institutional relationships between the state and the scientific research establishment.

The unusual position of Muriel Bell, a woman doctor directing a government research department, owes much to her dedication and determination, and something to the common ground between nutrition and what was then known as home science. The overlap between the feminised role of women in the kitchen and the goals of nutritional science opened up the scientific field of nutrition to women. In the decades after World War II, however, as the nation prospered, health priorities changed: measures to address poverty and malnutrition seemed superfluous, and the doctrine of individual responsibility for one's well-being superseded state intervention. Nutrition no longer stood at the centre of medical and public health research, and now the strong feminisation of the field worked against it, leading to its ultimate devaluation. This trend was reflected in the disestablishment of the Nutrition Research Unit with which Muriel had identified strongly for much of her career. She felt the decision as a crushing professional and personal blow.

*

Muriel Bell's life provides an illuminating view of the history of public health and health research in New Zealand, but the converse is less true. She left very little in the way of personal diaries or letters, leaving the biographer with only a collection of anecdotes and brief, vivid glimpses of experiences that beg for elaboration. Even close colleagues from later years were unable to share many insights into her personality or her life. They knew her first and foremost in her capacity as director of the Nutrition Research Unit, and this professional relationship defined the terms of their friendship.

It is hard to write a life mainly from the public record, supplemented with some oral testimony from family members, friends, former colleagues and students. Even the tenor of Muriel Bell's early life in a pioneering community is difficult to gauge from local and family histories. We can discover little, for example, about how the early deaths of two siblings and her mother might have affected her. She married twice, both times to men many years older than she was; beyond the knowledge that they, most unusually for the time, took on the primary housekeeping duties, we know little about those relationships. Her own death is equally enigmatic: if she indeed took her own life, as a family member has suggested, she left only the most cryptic of clues.

It is fortunate that Muriel's social connections from the early part of her adult life include such political figures as Peter Fraser and Walter Nash, which suggest a direct connection to national leaders and decisionmakers. Her friendship with the pacifist Millicent Baxter and other educated women places her in the company of committed leaders in their respective fields.

Muriel Bell distinguished herself early in her career with her unconventional (and practical) ways of doing things, whether by hurrying to patients' houses by bicycle during her medical studies in Dunedin or improvising methods of chemical analysis while working at a remote sheep station. Anecdotes from those who knew her show that she was also unconventional in her behaviour and mannerisms. One of her students at Otago Medical School commented that she gave the impression of a very active bird.[2] Her stepdaughter cited her as an example of how 'scientists were all queer'.[3] Her characteristic style of dress, a smock paired with open-toed sandals, revealed a woman with no conventional concern for her appearance. Ultimately, Muriel just did things her way.

*

My choice to use different forms of Muriel Bell's name reflects both the nature of this work and her own preferences. In a biography, it would be too impersonal to use only her family name; yet referring to her only by her given name would be a disservice to her professional standing. To mark copies of her board reports and scientific literature, Muriel used the initials MEB. Her publications appeared under the name of Dr Muriel E. Bell. During her marriage to her first husband, Jim Saunders, she adopted her husband's name for use in private life. Following her second marriage, to Alf Hefford, she used the name Muriel Hefford in official personal documents only. She identified most strongly as Dr Muriel Bell.

Chapter One

A PIONEERING SPIRIT

Muriel Bell once described the secret to her success in nutrition research: 'The way to pioneer a new subject is to have a pioneer lineage, on both sides of the family!'[1] Muriel's maternal grandfather, John Sheat, a twenty-two-year-old from Boltonsborough, near Glastonbury in Somersetshire, was one of the first immigrants to arrive in Nelson, aboard the *Mary Ann* in February 1842.[2] On her father's side, the Bell family was descended from pioneer settlers who had arrived in New Zealand in the 1840s. One of Muriel's great-grandfathers, William Gordon Bell, had managed a slave plantation on the Caribbean island of Carriacou. When the owner, Dr Bell (no known relation) died, William married his widow, Alziere Cervantes Bell. After the abolition of slavery, the business was no longer economical, and they returned to Scotland. Alziere's mother was West Indian, and Muriel was very proud of the features she had inherited from her great-grandmother.[3]

William and Alziere had five children. James, the eldest, wanted to go to New Zealand as a surveyor when the first New Zealand Company settlements were being planned. The whole family decided to emigrate, and they sailed from Liverpool on 17 July 1839.[4] After abandoning a plan to buy land in Australia, the family settled in Wellington in early 1840. William Gordon Bell attempted to farm wheat on Miramar Peninsula, in present-day Wellington.[5] He later drove cattle to Wanganui, but the New Zealand Company persuaded settlers in the area to choose land in the Nelson settlement.[6] William took on a sheep run in the Motupiko Valley.[7]

Muriel once recounted the story of her grandparents' introduction: her grandfather, James Bell, 'met the immigrant ship and asked Rev Dr

Thomas Burns whether there was anyone on board who would do for a wife for him. "There's Mary Ann Caradus – she is a good, God-fearing girl" was the reply, and that was how grandfather and grandmother came to be wedded.'[8] On 11 December 1848 Dr Burns married the couple in Dunedin, after which they returned to farm in the Nelson area and had one daughter and seven sons.[9]

Muriel's father, Thomas Bell, and his brother James purchased a farm at Four Rivers Plain near Murchison in 1885. Small-scale goldmining and bush farming were the main settler occupations, later supplanted by dairy farming.[10] The brothers also operated a sawmill on their land. Productive farming on the small area of flat land at the junction of the Buller, Matakitaki, Mangles and Matiri rivers proved challenging. Murchison was a settlement for the hardy.[11] The bush-covered hills were clad in fog and damp, especially in winter, and the remoteness of the area meant that communications were poor.

Thomas Bell married Eliza Sheat, the youngest of seven children of Eliza Avery and John Sheat, on 13 April 1886 in Richmond, and the couple settled on the family farm at Four Rivers Plain. Their first child, Francis Gordon (Frank), was born in 1887, followed the next year by Mary, who died in infancy. Elsie Grace was born in 1889 with the aid of Mrs Rosser, the local midwife. According to family history, the look on Mrs Rosser's face when she saw a 'bluish babe with the cord around its neck' made Eliza Bell burst into laughter.[12] Leslie George was born in 1892 and Arthur Wallace in 1894. Muriel Emma was born on 4 January 1898. The old family cottage had by then become too small for the family and needed repairs. Using native timber from the Bells' own sawmill, the family built a large, square, two-storey house, in which Muriel was brought up. Her younger sisters, Christina Sylvia (Chris) and Jessie, were born in 1902 and 1906 respectively.

Pioneering life in Murchison was still rough in the early years of the twentieth century. Roads were few, and rivers had to be forded on horseback. Farming, dredging and gold mining were the main industries. Thanks to the presence of Chinese gold miners in the river valleys, the Bell children remembered the excitement of receiving exotic treats of 'orange coloured fruit, nuts and Chinese ginger' at the times of Chinese festivals.[13]

The Bells were 'among the most prominent citizens of Murchison'.[14] They seemed to epitomise the observations of the Fabian socialists Beatrice and Sidney Webb during their visit to New Zealand in 1898: 'A people characterised by homely refinement, and by a large measure of vigorous public spirit.'[15] Thomas Bell represented Hampden Riding on the Inangahua County Council for eighteen years. (In 1882 Hampden was renamed Murchison, to avoid confusion with Hampden in Otago.) He was a member of the Licensing Bench, the school committee and 'in fact, of every public movement for the advancement and development of the district'.[16] As a prominent public figure, he presided at local sports events and concerts.[17] He was 'looked upon as the strong man of the district, not only in regard to public matters, but in regard to the health and general welfare of the settlers'.[18]

Thomas and Eliza Bell played important roles in Murchison's Methodist community, where they were known for their energy and hospitality. Thomas Bell had been a preacher in the church at Hope, where he had farmed with his brother James before moving to Murchison in 1885.[19] He converted to Methodism when he married Eliza and became a lay preacher.[20] In this role he sought to uphold religious values in the sometimes disorderly gold mining community. He refused to conduct a burial service, for example, unless the friends of the deceased promised to refrain from drinking beforehand.[21]

Thomas and Eliza were active in founding the interdenominational Sunday school, which started in the early 1890s and was attended by most settler children. Eliza was its first organist. Although the Methodist church was not built until 1914, long after Thomas Bell left the district, its congregation acknowledged him as one of its founders. In the foyer of the church is a mounted plaque in memory of 'circuit steward, trustee and local preacher, Thomas Bell'.

Murchison's remoteness forced the community to be largely self-reliant. The nearest health services were in Nelson, a day-long journey by horse – too far for many patients to travel. Accidents involving heavy machinery and harsh conditions were often fatal. Thomas Bell offered the community his self-taught medical and rudimentary surgical skills, using his own set of surgical and dental tools. Local newspapers recorded his skill in dressing wounds, as in as one case from the 1890s when a worker had two fingers crushed on a dredge.[22] When a young man suffered a bad fracture while breaking in a young horse, Thomas Bell set the limb to enable the patient to drive to Nelson.

The McNee family must have been especially grateful to Thomas Bell, for on two occasions he helped to save the lives of family members. When Robert McNee suffered life-threatening complications from a shoulder injury, Thomas Bell fought for a week to save him. They were great friends and often played chess and discussed politics and local affairs in the McNee home while waiting for the mail to arrive. When McNee's son Frank fell ill with appendicitis and required surgery to save his life, Thomas Bell administered the anaesthetic, while the local midwife, Mrs Rosser, assisted the doctor from Nelson with the operation. In the care of Thomas Bell and Mrs Rosser, Frank recovered well. Thomas was also known for extracting aching teeth.

Muriel herself enjoyed good health, which she attributed to both her parents: 'The honour goes to my mother who gave me a strong body, and to my father who acquired a great deal of medical knowledge from reading medical books – there was no doctor within 70 miles [112km], and he used to be a sort of doctor for the district we lived in, so I had the benefit of cod liver oil and such like in my childhood.'[23] In later life, Muriel marvelled at her father's scientific acumen in dosing his children with cod-liver oil for colds and sore throats.[24] 'No one knew at that time that it contained vitamin D which our food is lacking but which we can make for ourselves if there is enough sunshine. It was often very foggy where we lived in Murchison.'[25]

As Murchison's population grew, the community sought ways to attract a qualified doctor and formed a medical association. Members paid an annual subscription to subsidise the doctor's salary and received free treatment in return; non-members paid twice as much. In 1906, the association successfully appointed a Dr Howard. Despite its sparse membership, it continued until the Murchison County Council and Nelson Hospital Board took over responsibility for health services.[26]

It is difficult to say whether Eliza Bell shared her husband's enthusiasm for medicine and science. She did not have access to the type of education in homemaking recommended by the Women's Christian Temperance Union, which included the study of chemistry, physics, hygiene, architecture, art, music and childcare.[27] Eliza was, however, active in local charitable enterprises. As local agent for the Reefton Benevolent Society, she 'attended the needs of the less fortunate'.[28] The society organised fundraising events in Murchison, and Eliza was a popular performer at the charity concerts. She 'took the keenest possible interest in relieving distress'.[29] Her children frequently joined her on her rounds to deliver charitable aid.[30]

Muriel's late childhood was clouded by losses. In early 1905 her eldest brother, Francis, whom she resembled greatly, became acutely ill with appendicitis. He was transferred to the hospital in Nelson, where he underwent an operation and remained for some months. After a second operation in August, although he seemed to be improving, 'he suddenly sank and died'.[31] In 1906 her sister Jessie was born. Described as a 'frail little girl', she was entrusted to Muriel's care.[32] Jessie had an alimentary canal abnormality that caused great distress whenever she took any food, and which Thomas Bell's limited medical knowledge was powerless to alleviate. She died before her first birthday, and her passing affected the whole family deeply. 'Muriel particularly was absolutely devastated, and she used to recall how the Reverend Thomas Fielden Taylor tried so hard to comfort her.'[33] Her powerlessness to save Jessie may have contributed to her future willingness to drop everything to help a mother and child in need. According to her brother Wallace, Muriel's lifelong loathing of funerals also stemmed from this time.[34] Jessie's funeral incorporated Victorian rituals of mourning: four little girls were the pallbearers, wearing white dresses, black sashes and black hair ribbons.[35]

Devastatingly, the Bells had to endure another death in the family. On top of mourning two of her children, Eliza burnt herself badly while doing the washing in a copper tub.[36] For backblock districts such as Murchison, washing machines and other household appliances were still a generation away. It appeared that Thomas – who may also have been unwell at this time, as the *Buller Post* reported news of his illness – decided to take his wife on a convalescent trip, taking in the 1906 Christchurch Exhibition and leaving the children in the care of a local resident.[37]

The route to Christchurch in those years involved travelling first to Wellington and thence by ferry to Lyttleton. On the return journey from Christchurch, the Bells spent the day in Wellington. On 3 May 1907, after visiting friends in Brooklyn, they were on board tram number 55 at 5.30pm when it ran off the rails and capsized near Nairn Street on the Brooklyn Hill. All on board sustained injuries. A journalist's report stated: 'Mrs Bell was killed outright, her body being found in a badly mangled condition half in and half out of the car. Mr Bell is not able to give any clear account of the actual mishap. He escaped with a severe bruising and cut hand and bad shock. He was found clear of the car on the side opposite the track.'[38] An enquiry into the accident revealed that the 'reversing lever had been placed in the wrong position, causing the magnetic brake to become inoperative'.[39]

News of the tragedy reached Murchison by telegraph. The postmistress, Jessie McNee, saddled her horse and crossed the Matakitaki River to the Bells' farm to deliver the terrible news. Eliza Bell was so well known for her 'kindliness and generosity' throughout the district that in noting her death, the reporter for Murchison felt it 'quite unnecessary … to recapitulate her many esteemed qualities in this place'.[40] Another tribute described her as 'the personification of hospitality … her home was ever open to visitors.'[41]

After the accident, Thomas Bell remained in Wakefield for some months to recuperate and then decided to leave the district. It is possible that his health had deteriorated. The *Nelson Evening Mail* reported: 'In rendering aid in a serious accident necessitating his standing in the cold waters of the Buller for several hours in winter time, that brought on a severe attack of pleurisy, which resulted in permanent injury to his health that forced Mr Bell to leave a fine property at Murchison and settle in the milder climate of Richmond.'[42] Apparently he never returned to the farm.[43] His close friend Edward Kidd, from Richmond, went to Murchison and sold the house and land on his behalf.[44]

On 29 October 1907, a notice in the *Buller Post* recorded the district's farewell to the Bell children:

> The elder scholars of the Murchison Sunday School met with Misses Bell and Master Bell at the Boyes' residence on Friday evening last to bid

> them farewell before leaving the district. On their arrival the guests were presented with dainty buttonholes of forget-me-nots, the scholars present expressing their deep regret at having to part with their old and dear schoolmates. After a very lively evening was spent in music and merry games the gathering closed by clasping hands and singing 'Auld Lang Syne'.[45]

It is impossible to know how the multiple deaths in her immediate family affected Muriel's development. Perhaps her love of learning served as an escape from loss and mourning, for her intellectual progress did not suffer.

In Richmond, Thomas Bell had purchased a lovely home on the hill, a large, single-storey house with views toward Mount Arthur in the west and over Tasman Bay in the north.[46] The property consisted of 100 acres (40ha) of land and extensive orchards and gardens.[47] Thomas married Jessie McNee, the Murchison postmistress, in September 1909. How they carried out their courtship remains unclear. Despite having only two years of formal schooling, Jessie McNee had led a busy life not only as postmistress but also as gold buyer, registrar of births, deaths and marriages and accountant for her father, Robert McNee. After marrying Thomas Bell, she appears to have taken on a full-time domestic role. In addition to his five children, Jessie and Thomas had two children, Jean Caradus in 1910 and May Alzie in 1916.

Once settled in Richmond, Thomas Bell again involved himself in public affairs. He became a member of the Richmond Borough Council, the Nelson Harbour Board and the Nelson Hospital and Charitable Aid Board in 1910. He was also an active Methodist lay preacher on the Richmond circuit. He eventually became mayor of Richmond on 2 May 1917, eleven days before his sudden death.

Family life in Richmond offered the dual advantages of excellent colleges in Nelson and farm life at home. Muriel was later grateful to have had a household and farming background that gave her an understanding of housekeeping and kitchen affairs, such as baking bread, cooking meals and preserving, as well as of 'the problems besetting the farmer who has to get the milk on to your table, day in, day out, 365 days of the year'.[48] During her teenage years Muriel insisted on being allowed to go and help milk the cows:

> They gave me an easy milker, but she had the unfortunate fault that she was a good kicker, and when she landed me out in the yard, I wasn't so keen on milking! At a later stage, preparing the cow by leg roping, washing, then putting on the cups, made me familiar with the routine by which cleanliness in handling the cow, and the machines and equipment makes all the difference to the quality of the milk. This has been important in the function I served on the Central Milk Council, as watch-dog for the quality of town milk.[49]

When investigating the nutritional importance of soil minerals early in her research career, Muriel often thought of a pet lamb that used to follow her to school. 'It had so much wool it could scarcely see out of its eyes. It had a much better fleece than one usually saw on the back of a sheep.' Muriel speculated on whether the matipo hedge that she used to feed it might have contributed 'something like a trace mineral, brought by the matipo from the depths of the soil'.[50]

While living in Murchison, according to her brother Wallace, Muriel was a very reluctant pupil: at first he and his older brother Leslie had to drag her all the way to school. The headmaster, Mr Huddlestone, taught elementary subjects. His beautiful handwriting was passed on to the children of Murchison. Both Muriel and Chris inherited pleasing singing voices. Miss Webb, who later taught sewing and singing, would often appeal to Muriel in singing class to 'sing up, Muriel, I rely on you'. [51]

Because of Muriel's aptitude for learning, Thomas Bell sought out the best available school for her. In 1907 she began travelling by train with her brothers Leslie and Wallace to attend Nelson Girls' Central School. Under the instruction of Fido W. Knapp, the headmaster, Muriel won a junior national scholarship in her last year. She enrolled in Nelson Girls' College as a day girl in 1911.

In her first year at college she became very ill with scarlet fever, and her stepmother nursed her at home. Jessie McNee was 'meticulously careful in her infection-nursing technique', taking great care not to infect anyone; and indeed, no one else in Richmond contracted the disease at the time.[52] The other children were sent to stay with friends and relatives while Muriel recovered. In one of the columns she later wrote for the *Listener*, Muriel recalled being given baked custard during her illness. She traced 'her perfectly irrational dislike for a good food' back to this period: 'The memory is still so strong of that slippery feeling that even now it lingers.'[53]

Muriel soon returned to college and resumed her academic success, becoming head girl in 1915 on the basis of her scholastic achievements. Her memories of her college days included botany expeditions up Dun Mountain and to the reservoir, listening to stories during sewing lessons, Mr Lemmer's singing lessons, learning to appreciate the classical pictures that decorated the walls, and the excitement over the plays and concerts. While in London in 1933, she recalled that her most persistent memory of her schooldays was simply 'the walk to and from school, with spring budding and summer glowing with varying light and shade on land and water'.[54]

Despite her academic attainments, Muriel felt a sense of terror in writing 'the essay on what we wanted to be when we grew up. Some of us had not even nebulous ideas of what we wanted to become, and merely filled the pages with pious hopes which earned for us the premature designation of idealists.'[55] Even for bright pupils like Muriel, higher education for girls seemed to be out of reach. She recalled in the school's jubilee publication of 1933 'how unattainable we thought were University degrees. We wondered whether we should ever be able to climb to the heights of a B.A.'[56] By her own admission, it was 'rather a surprise to me and also a surprise to my family' when she was awarded a university scholarship.[57] Having excelled in languages at school, she began an arts course at Victoria University College, Wellington, in 1916.

At the time when Muriel was considering her future, opportunities were increasing for women in the sciences. Professors Ann Strong and Gertrude Rawson arrived from the United States to start up the School of Home Science at the University of Otago in 1911. This American academic duo quickly subverted the original impetus for women's education in domestic science (a technological solution to the shortage of domestic servants) to create a professional science training centre. This signalled a move toward the application of scientific principles in the home and new goals for teaching science in girls' schools.

World War I was to have long-lasting and unforeseeable effects on Muriel's future. She later recalled her feelings on learning that the British Empire was going to war:

> I shall not forget with how little of the prevailing excitement I went up to the sixth form room on the morning of August 4th, 1914, and felt somehow contrite that the British Empire was going to be involved in a war. 'You're not patriotic', was the greeting. Soon, however, the wave of patriotism submerged us all; we busied ourselves with making clothes for Belgian refugees, socks (rather heteromorphic socks) for soldiers, and were restrained in our zeal only by the Lady Principal's epigram that 'knitting is an excuse for idleness'. Our essay during that first week in August was on the subject that 'War is not an unmixed evil', and we wrote of the enervating effects of peace, and of the way in which war brings out the latent qualities of heroism and self-sacrifice. To-day, one feels much more inclined to write a bitter essay on the sterility of War.[58]

Muriel's brother Leslie was a medical student at Otago University when World War I broke out in August 1914. He interrupted his studies to join the Expeditionary Forces, which landed in Gallipoli in 1915. He was a sergeant (and later a lieutenant) in the medical corps and served in the NZ Field Ambulance Corps in Gallipoli. The following year, the army corps removed him from active service because of severe diarrhoea: he was admitted to a base hospital in Alexandria and then to St David's Hospital in Malta with jaundice. Later, in Cairo, the corps discharged him as unfit for duty and sent him back to New Zealand to finish his medical degree.[59] On hearing that Muriel had started university, Leslie wrote suggesting that she should do a medical course. Muriel wrote 'a very careful letter to her father asking what he thought of the idea. He was delighted and telegraphed his wholehearted approval.'[60] In a later interview, she speculated that at the 'back of his ready consent was his own thwarted desire to be a doctor'.[61]

Chapter Two

MEDICINE AS A CAREER PATH

Like many young women of her era interested in studying medicine, Muriel initially aspired to be a medical missionary. This was an acceptable career choice for women: it provided a safe outlet for intellectual ambition by subsuming it under the ideal of service to others. Her close friend in later years, Marion Robinson, claimed: 'Dr Bell did become a medical missionary, but in a somewhat unusual way – as a home missionary bringing good nutrition to everyone throughout New Zealand.'[1]

Muriel's 'moment of revelation' about her future was her brother Leslie's return from serving overseas.[2] World War I was a catalyst for the entry of many women into the medical profession. They cemented the path staked out by former graduates such as Emily Siedeberg, the first woman in New Zealand to graduate in medicine; Margaret Cruickshank, the first woman to graduate with the New Zealand degree of doctor of medicine; and Marion Whyte, who travelled overseas to specialise in anaesthesia. Muriel's university education came at a time of both horror at the senseless wartime destruction of human life and hope for a better future. This optimism accompanied Muriel as she entered the medical profession.

The application of medicine to populations rather than individuals – public health – became an ambitious social project. Born of the worldwide influenza epidemic in 1918, the 1920 New Zealand Public Health Act played an important part in the nation's modern social vision. It reflected the rapid growth of knowledge and expertise in medical sciences and the increasing role of medicine and medical professionals in the lives of citizens. The speech of one doctor at a meeting of the Empire Service

League demonstrated the enthusiasm with which medical leaders in far-flung corners of the empire embraced the all-pervasive notion of public health. Dr Colquhoun emphasised the lessons of World War I in preventing infant mortality and childhood disease. He extolled the virtues of 'the demonstrated efficiency of modern methods', including fresh-air schools and other hygienic measures.[3]

Medical women played a key part in widening the scope of medical science to encompass the health of women, children and families. They held key public health positions through new institutions such as the School Medical Service, the School Dental Service and health camps. Started in 1919, health camps aimed to combat child malnutrition, which was associated with tuberculosis.[4] Under the supervision of Dr Elizabeth Gunn (a known eugenicist), the health camp movement enacted the principles of good hygiene, healthy diet, fresh air and physical activity by sending children to country or seaside locations for summer holidays. Dietary principles were represented as affordable and simple to follow. Unfortunately for the health camp attendees of the later 1920s, the implementation of these principles shifted from the administration of chocolate to a less palatable source of important vitamins, cod-liver oil. One child recalled the compulsory three helpings of porridge, then a teaspoon of cod-liver oil, followed by a handful of raisins to take away the taste.[5]

Women medical professionals often specialised in treating women and children through these programmes. In part, this emphasis was seen as socially appropriate; but government public health positions also assured them some security of employment. In this regard they benefited from a national fervour to rebuild the nation and the population after the devastating losses of the war. An enthusiasm for racial fitness placed a new emphasis on the role of women in the family.

The Plunket Society, established under the guidance of Dr Truby King in 1907, advocated scientific solutions to the problems of child rearing, in keeping with the emergence of 'a radically more industrial or modern society'.[6] The medical profession sought ways to curb infant and maternal mortality rates. Education lay at the foundation of the movement, with volunteer women's groups helping to disseminate information on child nutrition and rearing. The 'ideology of scientific motherhood' represented a turn away from traditional practices passed down from generation to generation and toward a future in which the development of young New Zealanders was scientifically guided from the moment of birth.[7] As 'modern' mothers dedicated more time and effort to raising their children, they sought advice from Plunket nurses.[8]

This ethos also emphasised the role of housework and the home in ensuring the health and happiness of the family. Medicine was enlisted in the cause of efficiency and regeneration after the extreme loss of human life in the war. Overall, this growing confidence in science and its potential to improve the lives of citizens influenced the new generation of doctors, giving them a strong faith in public health and a dedication to bettering society.

University life in Dunedin

Women medical students were still unusual in the early twentieth century, but their numbers were rising. Muriel was one of 'a close and friendly group of seven or eight women among only 30 students in all' who began their medical training at the University of Otago, New Zealand's only medical school, in 1917.[9]

The start of her studies was marked, however, by the loss of her father, whose medical knowledge had influenced her career choice. On the evening of 13 May 1917, Thomas Bell went about his usual affairs. He conducted a service at the Brightwater Methodist Church before returning home and retiring to bed. That night he died from a severe stroke.[10] Muriel learned the devastating news the following day.[11] Soon afterwards, Jessie Bell disposed of the house and land at Richmond and returned to Murchison to live with her parents. This decision may have been driven by financial necessity, as Thomas had taken out mortgages on various pieces of land he had bought.[12] Certainly the Bell children received little money to support their studies.[13] Thereafter Muriel had little contact with her stepmother and devoted herself to her university studies.

Although money was short, Muriel had family support in Dunedin. Her brother Leslie was finishing his final year of medical school at Otago

University in 1917, and in 1921 her younger sister Chris came to Dunedin. She intended to train as a teacher but soon enrolled at Otago University, where she excelled in mathematics. Muriel's cousin Raynor Bell was appointed chair of clinical dentistry at Otago University in 1920. He was the first to obtain the degree of doctor of dental surgery from a New Zealand university and, according to a colleague, showed 'an aptitude for research bordering almost on genius'.[14] His wife, Yetti Bell, had also been a medical student for three years during World War I, but she ceased her studies once she became engaged, partly for financial reasons. Thereafter she became 'rather conventionally domestic for a little while' before pursuing a career as a music teacher.[15] Muriel's association with her cousin's family proved to be long-lasting and loving.[16]

Muriel's early political ideas were shaped by the conservative stance of her parents, a position based on loyalty to pioneering communities and colonial society. But once she left home and entered Otago Medical School, her mind opened to new ideas about the world and her place in it. She was drawn to Christian socialism, which combined traditional moral values and a sense of community with more radical ideas about social equality. The Christian Left was popular with young educated men and women who hoped for a new society based on internationalism and peace.[17] The 1917 Russian Revolution sparked a fervour for creating a new world and social order.

Muriel was an active member of the Christian Union during her days as a medical student. She attended a Bible study circle whose activities included a close reading of such books as Walter Rauschenbusch's *Social Principles of Jesus* and J.H. Oldham's *Studies on the Teachings of Jesus,* and raising money for Russian and European student relief. At a conference of the Christian Union in Geraldine in 1920, men and women who had the privilege of university education were called upon 'to take up the responsibilities of citizenship. This demands a thorough understanding of the problems of the day, and offers a challenge to every true student to consecrate himself to the business of life with a seriousness worthy of men and women who cherish the highest ideals.'[18] Its leaders called on those attending to join in their aim to 'discover the mind of Christ' on the problems of today, to see 'the true realities of life' and find 'a new passion for serving, and a new ideal of service.'[19] Pacifist discussions were common at such conferences.[20] Muriel appears to have been an active member until 1920, and her sister Chris became involved at the executive level in 1922–23.

Although Muriel's affiliation with Christian socialism as a student was short-lived – her friends in later life remembered that she had little time for religion – she maintained a lifelong commitment to pacifism. She remained politically to the Left, and her private book collection showed a leaning toward the writings of Fabian socialists, especially George Bernard Shaw. While Muriel may have dispensed with their ideologies, she certainly retained a strong sense of their values, especially the collective spirit of socialism, its internationalism and ideals of service. It was also through the peace movement that Muriel met James Saunders, her future husband.

In 1917–18 Muriel's residential college, St Margaret's College, had a higher complement of medical students than in previous years. Of a total of sixty students, twenty-two were studying medicine and teaching, with the remaining students in the faculties of arts, massage (physiotherapy), science and home science. Among the medical students were some who became her lifelong friends: Augusta (Gusty) Kippel (later Manoy), Elaine Gurr and Frances McAllister (later Preston). The Otago Medical School historian Dorothy Page notes that women medical students maintained networks of personal friendships and support long after their student days.[21] This 'inner circle', bonded by gender as well as medical training, provided a supportive environment, academic mentoring and enduring friendship.[22]

To a large extent, the sense of community emerged from communal meals and the rite of filling up hot-water bottles and gathering around the urn on wintry nights at a latitude of 45 degrees south.[23] Dr Marion Whyte 'pointed out that a college did for a university what the university could not do for itself. It provided a means of living together and talking together, and developed an atmosphere of thought and discussion.'[24]

Otago University was the only New Zealand university with a medical school and also the only university with a school of home science. In home science, women were not simply tolerated within a male sphere:

they were in control. Home science students studied alongside medical students. Professor Ann Strong emphasised that the curriculum consisted of more than instruction in cooking and sewing: 'The girl of to-day needs primarily to know the principles governing healthful living for herself, her family, and her community … Her growing privileges in social and political life demand of her training which will develop interest in civic and national affairs. She needs to be taught the relation of the modern home to all these economic, social, scientific, aesthetic and spiritual problems.'[25]

Amid concerns about the lack of student participation in university life, Muriel was omnipresent in student societies. In addition to the Christian Union, she was a member of the Bible Study Group, the Otago University Students Association (OUSA) and the Women's Faculty Association. The increasing number of female students at Otago University led to greater representation and inclusion of women in the university student associations. A revised OUSA constitution came into force in September 1920, under which Muriel was the first 'Lady Vice-President'. She served on the Social Committee and the Capping Ball Committee in 1920–21, and her contribution to the success of the events merited special mention in the *Otago University Review*.[26]

While social activities were an important part of their function, university organisations also provided places where students could develop their ideas about society, politics and their paths toward personal fulfilment. An important society for women students was the Women's Faculty Association. In its early years this organisation focused on organising social events, such as 'kahanga' and dances. Kahanga were strictly feminine entertainment, 'no rules – dress-as-you-please, fancy or otherwise, a free-for-all evening'.[27] Women medical students often volunteered for positions on the committee. Muriel first sat on the committee during her third year at medical school in 1919. The reconstitution of OUSA effectively rendered the Women's Faculty Association defunct; it was replaced by the Women's Club in 1920.

The Women's Club had wider-ranging objectives for service to the community and more ambitious academic goals for its members than the previous association.[28] Its constitution of 1921 specified its objects:

to further social activities among all students, to promote intellectual cooperation among the various faculties, and to promote the interests of the women of the university.[29] The professors of home science, Ann Strong and Gertrude Rawson, were leading figures in the club and role models for the interwar generation of young university women: formidable and intelligent, as women had to be if they were to be taken seriously in a world still dominated by men. Rawson stated that 'education must mean general culture and the posterity of high ideals thus developing a wise balanced judgement'.[30] She called for the women present to 'find an ideal that will appeal to all types of University women for it is the ideal that inspires action'. Committees were set up immediately to investigate such issues as accommodation available to women students and their housing conditions.

Remaining prejudices

Despite the expansion of opportunities for university women, 'lady' medical students at Otago Medical School met with a mixed reception. Muriel's own recollections of her student days were that 'women were not altogether welcomed at the time, as medical students. Engraved on the desk that I sat in was the slogan "Women's place is in the home."' She mused, 'Perhaps it was the fact that we entered the course during the First World War when doctors were badly needed that made it easier for those who came after us.'[31]

Muriel's classmate Frances McAllister stated that 'our teachers on the whole took us for granted. Some obviously disapproved of women in medicine, but most were tolerant, some even liked us. But we had to be careful to give no cause for offence or criticism, and we worked hard – no girl could afford not to.'[32] Professor Lindo Ferguson, the dean of the medical school, was more obvious in his dislike for women students than other faculty members were. He made a point of addressing the class as 'gentlemen', refusing to acknowledge the women seated in the front row.[33] Muriel later recalled, in a newspaper interview about being a woman medical student in these years, that 'whenever anything went wrong it was always her fault – one more indication of prejudice'.[34]

The way their male counterparts received 'lady students' tells a similar tale. The Medical Students' Association refused women membership in 1920. Male students described them as having 'lost their pristine freshness', their femininity having 'wilted' and been replaced by 'masculine and slangy' talk. There existed, however, a gap between what women and men considered feminine. As early as 1922 university women saw medicine as a profession that was suited to their natural strengths and abilities.[35]

The new medical school, in the Lindo Ferguson Building, opened in April 1917 to accommodate larger numbers of medical students. Those who entered in 1917 were the last group to complete a five-year course of medical training; it was thereafter extended to six.[36] The first year focused on the elementary sciences of chemistry, biology and physics under Professors John Inglis, William Benham and Robert Jack respectively. Once past the first-year examination, students moved on to the dissection room, laboratories, and wards for anatomy and physiology instruction. The third year covered laboratory study of preclinical subjects: bacteriology under Sydney Champtaloup, pathology under A. Murray Drennan, systemic medicine under Dudley Williams Carmalt-Jones, clinical medicine under Frank Fitchett and surgery under Louis Barnett. The fourth year provided instruction in various specialties such as ophthalmology, obstetrics, radiology and anaesthesia before the final year of clinical instruction.

Muriel showed an early aptitude for scientific laboratory work. Frances McAllister recognised Muriel's scientific talent early on, as she and Muriel were work partners throughout their undergraduate careers. She remembered Muriel's approach as 'extremely careful and particular, overlooking no "source of error" or detail, however small. She [Muriel] arrived at results by reasoning and scientific method.'[37]

Of all the professors at the medical school, John Malcolm, the professor of physiology, had the most profound influence on Muriel's life. Malcolm had a special interest in metabolism and nutrition. He had trained in Berlin under Nathan Zuntz and in Edinburgh under Edward Albert Schaefer, both eminent in their respective fields of metabolism and endocrinology. Before arriving in New Zealand in 1905, he had published papers on the composition of foods. In New Zealand he investigated the caloric and vitamin content of New Zealand foods, such as kūmara, oysters, toheroa, muttonbirds (tītī) and a wide variety of New Zealand fish, for the New Zealand Institute. As a founding member of the Council of Scientific and Industrial Research, established in 1926, he promoted research on nutrition.

Prior to the discovery of vitamins, late-nineteenth-century scientists had identified protein, fats, carbohydrates, water and mineral salts as essential to the human diet. However, research demonstrated that these substances alone did not necessarily result in good health. The biochemists Christiaan Eijkman and Frederick Gowland Hopkins filled in part of this puzzle with their discovery of 'accessory food factors', or vitamins. Building on this knowledge, scientists were able to discover the aetiology of deficiency diseases such as rickets, scurvy, pellagra, beriberi and night blindness.

Muriel described the breadth of Malcolm's knowledge of physiology and medicine as 'astounding' and observed that his colleagues regarded him 'as much a pioneer of biochemistry as of physiology in New Zealand'.[38] Indeed, Malcolm also demonstrated an interest in pharmacology, as shown by his early publications on the native plant poison tutin. Once arrived at Otago, he focused his research on 'the New Zealand things like plant poisons, bush sickness and such like'.[39] Muriel's interest in investigating local problems was more than likely a result of Malcolm's influence.

Nutrition research began at Otago in 1922, under the umbrella of the New Zealand Institute of Research, when Malcolm arrived with twenty Wistar laboratory rats from Britain. On the ocean journey he travelled with the rats in his own cabin and attended personally to their feeding and care. By the time he arrived in New Zealand, there were sixty rats, causing 'some difficulties' with customs.[40]

Malcolm's teaching of physiology reflected his own view of research as a 'steadily developing matter with plenty more to be found out in every branch'.[41] The disciplines of endocrinology and nutrition emerged from physiology in the first decades of the twentieth century. Douglas Robb, a classmate of Muriel's, recalled Malcolm's lectures being 'remarkably up to date and somehow we understood and embraced the idea of working "with nature", which is "Physiology"'.[42] Malcolm was the first professor to use animals for his practical physiological teaching, such as wild rabbits for blood pressure measurements and frogs for muscle studies.[43] Muriel went on to replicate this practice in her teaching and research. In pharmacology lectures, the professor applied lessons drawn from Malcolm's physiological experiments.[44]

Muriel admired Malcolm's dedication to teaching during the applied physiology course in her fifth year, especially in the Saturday morning clinics, in which he outlined the physiological basis of a particular disease. The effort he put into these classes meant that graduates who went to England for further degrees were able to pass the primary fellowship examination without much additional effort.[45]

Muriel Bell spent her final year at medical school as a public health bursar. The scheme accepted eight bursars annually to live in at Dunedin Hospital (the only hospital with any accommodation for women), where they gained valuable experience by assisting house surgeons. In what was to be the final year of the scheme, 1921, Elaine Gurr and Muriel were the only women selected. Muriel worked under the supervision of William Newlands and P. McClymont.[46] Dr Newlands taught surgery at Otago Medical School and was an honorary staff member at Dunedin Hospital.

Elaine Gurr remembered the experience as 'arduous days' and commented that 'house surgeons made them work very hard'.[47] Bursars, like other students, had to attend lectures and complete practical work in addition to their hospital duties. There was no laboratory assistance for diagnostic testing: house surgeons and bursars did their own blood counts and urine tests on patients. Bursars were on duty every night and at weekends for calls to the wards, operating theatre and casualty department and were responsible for their supervisors' patients. Bursars also had to respond to emergency calls, often in the poorer parts of town, from patients who could not contact a general practitioner or were unable to pay the fee. One night when most of Dunedin's practitioners were attending a medical dinner, Muriel attended a call from Carroll Street:

> This area having a very bad name, the old Scottish porter, Davy Drysdale, was very worried and advised her to take a scalpel with her, but Dr McClymont showed her how to use a stick. Armed with this she sallied forth and caught a tram to the Exchange where she managed to collect a

> policeman with a torch. The man who had called the hospital was waiting up the hill past Sew Hoy's premises, and he led them down a lane for about fifty yards, along a row of cottages. In one of these houses the patient was sitting by the fire, wrapped in a blanket, and surrounded by neighbours, from whom came a surprised murmur of 'A lady doctor'.[48]

However great their astonishment may have been, it cannot have outweighed Muriel's own sense of pride and purpose in being a young woman practising medicine.

Chapter Three

RESEARCH: IN PURSUIT OF KNOWLEDGE

As a promising graduate, Muriel had more career choices available to her than many of her fellow Otago students. She chose to continue studying toward a research degree in medicine. This choice was open to her partly because of her exceptional skills in laboratory work and the support of Professor Malcolm, but it was also influenced by the limited opportunities for women doctors in the 1920s to practise their profession on patients. They stood little chance of selection for prestigious hospital positions.[1] The most lucrative choice was to go into private practice, especially with a day surgery, but here, too, opportunities were severely limited by prejudice against women in the profession and the financial investment required to join or establish a practice. Women doctors were therefore effectively pushed into specialties like anaesthesia and radiotherapy, where the hours were long and pay was low. The expansion of state-sponsored public health initiatives, however, had opened up new (if often dull) opportunities for women in the School Medical Service and other public health roles.

Among Muriel's peers, Margaret Cruickshank and Alice Horsley were successful in private practice, and others went into general practice with their husbands. Elaine Gurr and Ada Paterson pursued careers in the Department of Health, while Eleanor Baker-McLaglan chose employment in the School Medical Service, providing regular medical visits to primary schools. Some women were successful in paediatric and gynaecological fields, such as Emily Siedeberg, who became superintendent of St Helen's

Hospitals in Dunedin, and Doris Gordon, who practised obstetrics. Dr Winifred Bathgate established an ear, nose and throat clinic at Dunedin Hospital, and Caroline Stenhouse became an eye specialist after training at Moorfields Eye Hospital in London. Other women, like Frances McAllister, gave up their medical careers to marry and raise a family. Eschewing all of the more typical roles of the woman doctor or medical missionary, Muriel Bell opted to pursue a career in public health research.

Graduate life

By the time Muriel graduated from medical school in 1922, two important organisations had been established to support women graduates: the New Zealand Federation of University Women (NZFUW) and the New Zealand Medical Women's Association (NZMWA). The former brought graduates together to promote friendship and understanding, while the latter aimed to further the interests of medical women throughout New Zealand, in part through meetings at which its members presented papers.[2] At the August 1927 meeting, Muriel read a paper titled 'Some recent findings in physiology'. It dealt with the role of calcium in the blood, the regulation of blood calcium levels, the cause of tetany (muscle spasms frequently associated with low blood calcium) and its treatment with parathyroid hormone. She also touched on the principles of dieting for the treatment of gout and some of the new antiseptic drugs.[3]

Muriel's association with both organisations endured throughout her career. In 1924 the NZMWA became affiliated to the British Medical Women's Federation and the Medical Women's International Association (MWIA). NZMWA members travelling abroad enjoyed 'the privilege of introduction' to these societies. The MWIA's professed purpose was 'to form a united band of professional women working for the health and welfare of the world' and to foster 'the international co-operation in preventive medicine of men and women in [the medical] profession'.[4] This focus on social issues corresponded to Muriel's own vision. According to the MWIA's president, Lady Florence Barrett, medical women had a distinctive and valuable perspective on health issues. In the field of applied nutrition, for example, having women on a committee on food prices and values offered 'invaluable help and stimulus, because of their special contribution to the subject' owing to their domestic experience.[5]

Despite the persistent prejudice against women in the medical school, the shortage of male graduates during and immediately after World War I meant that top women graduates were often employed as teaching assistants. Although university positions were poorly paid, it was a time of 'unprecedented opportunity' for young female graduates.[6] In 1916 Doris Gordon became assistant in bacteriology, and in 1918 Grace Stevenson became assistant pathologist. Marion Whyte started teaching anaesthetics in 1921, and Gladys Cameron, having assisted Professor Champtaloup in teaching bacteriology and hygiene, took over his lectures during his illness in 1920–21.

Even with the return of male students to their studies after the war, which led to a sharp rise in the number of medical school graduates during 1923–24, Malcolm's physiology department was plagued by a shortage of assistants. The common attitude remained that 'there was little future in New Zealand for trained physiologists and little thought in the minds of students to regard Physiology as a portal to a higher diploma'.[7] For Muriel Bell, however, physiology proved to be the perfect training ground for a career in nutrition.

At the end of her medical course in 1922, Malcolm offered Muriel a position as his assistant, and she accepted. Shortly afterwards the head of surgery at Dunedin Hospital also offered her a position, which she declined.[8] Thus Muriel remained in the medical school demonstrating as a junior assistant in the physiology department. Later in life she cited this event as evidence that 'our destiny is often decided by narrow margins of time or circumstance'.[9] Rather than articulate her desire for a career in medical research, some thirty years later she still attributed her career choice to fate. Muriel began by assisting Malcolm in teaching and research work in the 'days when metabolism was assuming an increasingly important place in physiology'.[10]

Malcolm's influence on Muriel Bell's career is evident in multiple aspects of her later research profile. 'As his assistant', she later noted, 'I had access to the journals that told of the new discoveries that were going on in nutrition. And so I became interested in it myself.'[11] Furthermore, as Malcolm's assistant in the laboratory as well as the classroom, Muriel became informed about the research topics that interested Malcolm: 'It was only natural that I should follow his lead.'[12] Her responsibilities mirrored Malcolm's in a department that would be considered very short of personnel and technology by today's standards. Muriel, like Malcolm, did research, teaching and experimental work. She also fed his prized rat colony, established with the help of Muriel and the technician Harry Manson. The use of experimental animals had begun only in the 1920s at Otago Medical School, and feeding the rats was deemed a task appropriate to the expertise of his most talented postgraduate scholar.[13]

It was with strong encouragement from Malcolm that Muriel embarked on acquiring the degree of doctor of medicine (MD), a research qualification to which few medical graduates, men or women, aspired. 'I suppose it is true to say that I have been tempted all my life to go and bury my one little talent in the earth instead of making use of it, and I have had to goad myself into making use of it.'[14]

For her MD thesis, and her first major research project, Malcolm proposed the study of basal metabolism as a test of thyroid function, as a means of diagnosing the high number of goitre and thyroid surgery cases in New Zealand. Muriel recalled, 'Our hospital wards always contained some cases of thyrotoxicosis, or of unsightly enlargement, diffuse or adenomatous, of the thyroid gland, requiring surgery.'[15] The high incidence of the disease was attested by the common symptom of visible swelling of the neck and by medical statistics gathered from World War I army recruits. Charles Hercus, government bacteriologist and the chair of public health at Otago Medical School, led the research on the problem, conducting studies on schoolchildren, Karitane hospital nurses and Tūhoe iwi.[16] Chemical and geological investigations in the 1920s revealed that some areas of New Zealand, including Canterbury, have naturally low levels of iodine in the soil, which leads to iodine deficiencies in the human diet that can cause thyroid disease.

At the time, diagnosing thyroid disease was difficult because of the lack of clinical signs that provided a definitive diagnosis. The thyroid gland controls the body's metabolism, and common symptoms of an overactive thyroid, like an increased pulse rate, could also be attributed to a number of other causes, such as 'emotional imbalance' or 'neurasthenia' (particularly since the condition was more common in women), or 'thyrotoxicosis' (hyperthyroidism, also known at the time as toxic goitre). Before the function of thyroid hormones in the endocrine system was understood, it was believed that endemic and toxic goitre were related both aetiologically and therapeutically. There was considerable interest in the subject: six articles on goitre appeared in the *Proceedings of the University of Otago Medical School* in 1924.

In the United States, doctors often used a measurement of the basal metabolic rate (BMR) to diagnose the illness, but many New Zealand doctors were reluctant to accept the results as justification for surgically removing the thyroid.[17] Dr Stanley Batchelor, who performed much thyroid surgery in the Dunedin surgical clinic, was anxious to get the BMR test accepted in New Zealand. Muriel completed her initial study on BMR in her first year out of medical school, in 1922, after which the test was accepted as a diagnostic aid. By providing a better means of distinguishing toxic goitre from other forms of thyroid disease, her work saved many patients from the unnecessary removal of the thyroid gland. The project was the basis of her first research paper, 'Some studies in basal metabolism'.[18]

At times Muriel's research attracted attention and caused amusement. The BMR required estimating the patient's lowest metabolic rate, so Muriel travelled to patients' homes between 8am and 10am to carry out the test, having instructed them to eat no supper or breakfast and to lie in bed for a least an hour prior to the test. The test involved measuring the amount of carbon dioxide in a patient's exhaled breath, which allowed a calculation of calories burned – the metabolic rate. Muriel took the breath samples using a specially constructed mask that fed the air into a Douglas bag, 'a rubber-lined canvas bag capable of holding about 75 litres'.[19] Walking to the medical school from the hospital, 'her huge bag filled with the patient's expired air', Muriel must have been a hilarious sight.[20] Back at the physiology department, Muriel completed the analysis of the air.[21] Speed was imperative, so Muriel took to riding a bicycle. She recalled that 'one morning when she entered the courtyard of the Medical School, the professor of [systemic] medicine, Mr Carmalt-Jones, was there to greet her with the reprimand, 'Muriel this is pure affectation – riding a bicycle!'[22]

In 1923 she resigned as junior assistant to become a resident at Dunedin Hospital, under the supervision of Carmalt-Jones. Although it was not necessary for her professional qualification, Muriel may have thought that a year of postgraduate hospital training would keep the door open to future hospital positions. Still at an early stage in her career, Muriel was prudent in seeking out alternatives to her junior assistantship with Malcolm. Marion Radcliffe-Taylor and Muriel were appointed as two of eight house surgeons. Being the only women, they had separate living quarters: two rooms above the Central Hall of the main hospital building (built in 1866), among storerooms, records and sewing rooms; rats ran along the pipes in their rooms. Her Monday schedule leaves an impression of a busy and strenuous life: 'On Mondays, Dr Carmalt-Jones' clinical rounds did not finish till 4pm. Dr Bell then had to catch a tram to Kaikorai Valley, walk up the hill to Wakari [Hospital], do her rounds there, rush back to the Kaikorai terminus to catch a tram for town, and thence literally run to hospital, where she was on duty from 6pm, on call through the night for casualty and wards.'[23] House surgeons supervised students in the wards, showing them how to apply dressings and take blood samples. There was little funding for sharp needles or replacements, so Muriel remedied the situation in her typical do-it-yourself fashion by sharpening them herself.

Cases of infectious diseases filled the hospital wards in the early 1920s. Under Carmalt-Jones, Muriel was in charge of Miller Ward (medical), Miller Balcony (terminal tuberculosis cases), Isolation (diphtheria cases, many with complications) and Wakari Hospital, a sanatorium for long-term and advanced tuberculosis cases. Before the introduction of antibiotic treatment in the 1940s, Muriel often had to tell parents of children suffering from tuberculosis that 'there was no hope of recovery'.[24]

The terminal suffering Muriel witnessed during her residency influenced her decision to follow a career in research rather than medicine. When a research assistant asked her toward the end of her career why she had not chosen a traditional doctor's career, Muriel replied that she was tired of not knowing the answer to problems.[25] She saw the future of medicine as promoting health and preventing disease rather than simply alleviating symptoms. A fellow graduate of 1922, Charles Burns, commented on her experience:

> It was my impression that Muriel Bell did not much enjoy the role of House Physician or House Surgeon. Her sensitivity made it difficult for her readily to accept the rough and tumble life of resident medical staff of those days. Their numbers were very few and the duties so demanding and so variable as to make any kind of positive contribution almost impossible, except on a day to day basis, and I feel sure that she was more than happy to return, in the second year following qualification, to the quiet waters of the academic life, under her beloved Chief, Professor John Malcolm.[26]

Burns was assistant to the professor of pathology at the time. Another 1922 medical graduate, Douglas Robb, tutored in the Anatomy Department. With a shared interest in medicine, society and politics, the three formed a 'junior discussion club'.[27] Douglas Robb became a vocal critic of the government's medical service in the 1930s, publishing a number of pamphlets promoting alternative health care schemes. Muriel's interest in political issues became the basis of lasting friendships with many of her medical colleagues.

Taking the research pathway

Muriel returned to the Physiology Department as assistant lecturer in late 1923. At Otago, Malcolm continued the European tradition in medical research of having a protégé, and he proved influential in shaping her career. She received a grant from the Roberts Fund to continue her studies in basal metabolism.

Goitre research was the first major public health research project at Otago Medical School. Muriel's MD research on clinical patients with toxic goitre complemented the preventive work among schoolchildren by the professor of public health, Charles Hercus, and the school doctor Eleanor McLaglan-Baker. Their work in Canterbury, where thyroid disease was endemic, involved the experimental practice of giving iodine solutions to children with enlarged thyroids. While researchers overseas were conducting similar work, an increasing awareness of New Zealand's local conditions emerged, and with it the recognition of the need for additional research. Health professionals, geologists and chemists from the University of Otago worked together to investigate the geographical and social environment of Canterbury and its effect on human health. Similarly, public health experts sought local solutions to the goitre problem. The introduction of iodised salt had been successful in Switzerland, but New Zealand public health authorities were reluctant to introduce 'medicated' or 'adulterated' foodstuffs. Nutritional problems were fraught with uncertainty during the 1920s, as many new theories about deficiency diseases were coming to light in the wake of ground-breaking research on vitamins and minerals. Muriel would, however, return to the goitre problem when she became state nutritionist, advocating for the compulsory and cheap availability of iodised salt.

She completed her thesis, titled 'Clinical studies in basal metabolism in goitrous cases in New Zealand', graduating with the New Zealand MD degree in 1926. A photograph of her at the capping ceremony appeared in the *Otago Witness*.[28] In 1926 Muriel was the only woman in New Zealand to hold the MD degree. (Margaret Cruickshank, who had attained it twenty-three years earlier, died in Waimate while treating victims of the 1918 influenza epidemic.) The NZMWA recognised the significance of Muriel's achievement and congratulated her on attaining the degree at the organisation's 1927 annual meeting.[29] At the graduation ceremony Malcolm encouraged the dean, Lindo Ferguson, 'to say something to call attention to the fact that our women graduates seldom attain to that degree'.[30] Malcolm also wished to draw attention to the comments of the external examiner, Dr Blackburn of Sydney, in relation to Muriel's thesis: 'This is excellent and represents a large amount of ingenious work. It shows careful thought and sound judgment in regard to deduction. Will get first class MD.'

Despite this accolade, there had been a final hurdle to overcome: she was 3 per cent short of a passing mark on the written examination for the degree. In a letter urging that her grade be raised, Malcolm emphasised the excellent work Muriel had done for the hospital, 'involving a great deal of her time and for which she has not even received thanks'. Muriel had to put up with 'the apathy and even obstination' of the house staff. Often when she went to the hospital before 8am to conduct the BMR test, she found that no instructions had been given to prepare the patient for the test. In addition, Malcolm noted, she had to physically carry 'the large balloon-like bag of expired air' on the streets from the hospital to the Physiology Department because she would have had to pay for a taxi out of her own purse. Moreover, even after her thesis was completed, she had carried on doing the tests up to the date of her examination 'merely for the sake of helping others'. Malcolm believed that if she had spent this time preparing for the exam, she would have easily attained a passing mark. His letter also called attention to other inequities:

> The function of an internal examiner is to modify the opinion formed by the external examiner who judges the candidate merely on one examination. This he should be able to do from his personal knowledge of the candidate's abilities and clean record. Professor Carmalt-Jones made full use of Miss Bell's ability to determine metabolic rates both in Hospital and in his private practice and yet he is unable to allow her excellent thesis to counterbalance a deficiency of 3% in her paper while he raises the clinical marks of another candidate (Mackay) so as to allow him a pass.

Malcolm brought the issue before the faculty and called on the University Senate to rectify the 'miscarriage of justice' in denying her the MD degree. Although it is unclear how the situation was finally resolved, Muriel did indeed graduate with an MD.

She continued as a senior assistant in physiology until the end of 1927. But the Physiology Department at Otago University could never offer the vibrant research environment that overseas institutions could provide. When thinking back to his early days as a junior assistant in physiology, Norman Edson was left with the impression 'of large, empty rooms, many of which were seldom used'.[31] Malcolm, Bell and Edson were the only staff working in the department's premises in the new Lindo Ferguson Building. The only other staff member affiliated with physiology was Arini Pope, who was working on the nutritional composition of New Zealand foods, such as the vitamin content of New Zealand butter.

Postgraduate study in Britain was essential for New Zealand medical graduates wishing to distinguish themselves. London teaching hospitals provided the necessary experience to round out their medical knowledge. Large provincial hospitals were also thought to offer excellent and rigorous training, in part because the patient-to-student ratio was much higher than in the London teaching hospitals.[32] Postgraduate research work in New Zealand received little funding, and there was no support for research at the Otago Medical School until the formation of the Medical Research Council in 1937. In Britain, however, international medical women's publications promoted women's research work on rickets, vitamins and infant diseases.[33] With Malcolm's encouragement, Muriel applied for a research scholarship from the Royal Society of Medicine in April 1927. Although her application was unsuccessful, she was already planning to go abroad with Jim Saunders, her fiancé, to further her research career.

Born at Hamilton Station, Maniototo, in 1881, Saunders was eighteen years Muriel's senior. He had spent part of his life working in the coal mines on the West Coast of the South Island, the hotbed of radical socialism in nineteenth-century New Zealand. Many prominent left-wing Labour leaders emerged from this environment and refused conscription in World War I in resistance to the imperialist and capitalist aims of war.[34] Saunders was among them.

As a conscientious objector, he was sentenced to prison-camp labour planting trees, a punishment in every way preferable to the treatment of other conscientious objectors who went to jail or were sent to the front. He took great pride in his political convictions: when he took Muriel to the Kaingaroa state forest to show her the thirty-foot-tall pine and fir trees, he said, 'There, isn't that better than graves in Flanders?'[35]

Jim's political views and contacts meshed with Muriel's pacifism. The New Zealand Labour Party was closely aligned to the peace movement, and in the 1920s the Women's International League for Peace and Freedom was affiliated to the Labour Party and drew membership from its supporters.[36] In addition to endorsing pacifism, the league advocated for the interests of women, including motherhood endowment (a financial benefit for mothers), reducing maternal mortality, sex education and child welfare.

It is not clear precisely when Muriel and Jim Saunders met and began their courtship. Muriel and her sister Chris, who were flatting together, came into contact with many members of the intellectual Left who could have introduced the two.[37] They include Millicent Baxter, a well-educated friend of Muriel's who was married to the conscientious objector Archibald Baxter.[38] In her memoirs Millicent recalled meeting Peter Fraser, the future prime minister, in Muriel's home in 1924. Because Fraser was a friend of Jim Saunders, this suggests that Muriel and Jim might already have been well acquainted. It was common for pacifists, like communists, to meet in private houses for fear of being discovered by the police. Other mutual friends included Walter Nash and Arnold Nordmeyer.[39]

Muriel and Jim married at a relatively late age, perhaps because of Muriel's prolonged studies and the University of Otago's disinclination to employ married women (at least outside the School of Home Science). Jim's meagre income as a labourer would have been difficult for them to survive on, and it would have been nearly impossible for Muriel to raise a family while working full-time as a researcher. Their late marriage may also account for the fact that they had no children. When her niece Mona Randall asked her later in life whether she had ever wanted children, Muriel told her she could not have children, although she would have liked to have six.

On 10 January 1928 Jim and Muriel married at the registrar's office in Wellington, with Muriel's elder sister Elsie Bell, Peter Fraser, Jean Park (who trained as a teacher and was later appointed the first female Justice of the Peace) and Muriel's colleague Arini Pope as witnesses.[40] The marriage certificate recorded Jim as a labourer; Muriel's profession was not noted. They were in many ways an exceptional couple. Beyond the obvious differences in age, profession, education and status, Muriel's career took priority in their marriage, while Jim looked after their domestic life.

The annual report of the Dunedin branch of the NZMWA recorded Muriel's name change to Dr Muriel E. Saunders/Mrs Saunders, but she did not, in fact, use this name professionally.[41] She was one of the few women in New Zealand to use her maiden name publicly throughout her life, remaining Dr Muriel E. Bell. Her reasons for doing so are unclear. Because she had published only one paper under the name Bell in the *New Zealand Medical Journal* in 1923, changing her name would have caused no major break in her research profile. Because she was not an avowed feminist, it seems unlikely that her choice was a political stance against patriarchal conventions. Officially and in her private life she became Mrs James Saunders.[42]

Chapter Four

KNOWING BY INSTINCT

Shortly after marrying, Jim and Muriel travelled together to England and Europe. It was common for medical graduates to undertake three months of clinical training overseas toward the professional qualification known as a testimonial. An article in the *New Zealand Medical Journal* praised the standard of clinical work and training in Vienna, stating, 'It is a great deal more than a diploma mill'.[1] Muriel went there in 1928 to undertake clinical work, including studies of rachitic convulsions (seizures associated with rickets, a condition resulting from vitamin D deficiency), which were frequently seen in the children's wards.[2] Harriette Chick, a leading British researcher in biochemistry, had pioneered work on vitamin D deficiency during her clinical studies on rickets in Vienna after World War I.

While abroad, Muriel represented the New Zealand Medical Women's Association at the Medical Women's International Association conference in Bologna in 1928, convened under the patronage of Mussolini's Fascist Party.[3] The conference had two main topics: protection of the health of children and young persons, and diseases of the eye in relation to general medicine.[4] Muriel discovered that New Zealand had an excellent reputation for child welfare: 'When I was introduced to some of the German delegates, they told me that when going through their medical course, they had learnt that New Zealand was foremost in the world for the rights of the young.'[5] New Zealand's policies on sex education, venereal disease clinics and the role of women doctors in these clinics were of particular interest to conference participants.[6]

Muriel and Jim also visited London, another traditional destination for medical postgraduate study. Owing to a patriarchal backlash against women in the medical profession, however, by 1928 it had become nearly impossible for women to gain house appointments and clinical education in London hospitals or institutes.[7] Muriel sought posts at two prestigious medical institutions, University College (then part of the University of London) and the Lister Institute, but to no avail.[8] Nevertheless, she was able to gain experience in laboratory work at the Royal Free Hospital for Women in London before returning to New Zealand to take up a hospital position in Napier in 1929.

In her role as pathologist at Napier Hospital, in charge of the laboratory of the 250-bed hospital, Muriel's work was a combination of bacteriology and biochemistry. A contemporary article in a local newspaper on 'scientific women', referring to the bacteriologist as 'the bug hunter', could easily have described Muriel at work: 'Most of the hours that the day sends, she spends in the bacteriological laboratory of a New Zealand hospital. She is still very young – young enough to make her dark cloak and uniform of white piqué the trimmest things in the world – but neither youth nor uniform distracts her from work which most women would find rather gruesome.'[9] But Muriel's twelve-hour workdays left her little time for any research of her own.

Having been unsuccessful in her application for the Royal Society of Medicine's William Gibson Research Scholarship in 1927, she was delightedly surprised to learn that she had been awarded the scholarship in July 1929. The selection committee recorded in the minutes that 'amongst the considerations which led to the award was the fact that no award had as yet been made to a candidate from the Dominions. The Committee also felt that a candidate applying from overseas was not in so favourable a position as those who applied from Great Britain.'[10] Thus the nominal purpose of the scholarship, to support women researchers from parts of the empire other than Britain, was fulfilled. The scholarship allowed the recipient to choose where she worked. Muriel initially planned to leave as soon as possible to begin research at either the Lister Institute, under Sir Charles Martin, or University College, under Professor Jack Drummond. But the uncertainty surrounding Muriel's acceptance into either facility and the cost of travelling to and living in London led her to delay her departure.

In September 1929 at the request of Ernest Marsden, then secretary of New Zealand's Department of Scientific and Industrial Research (DSIR), Muriel agreed to carry out a six-week investigation into a sheep ailment called 'bush-sickness' or 'dopiness' on a farm at Piopio near Te Kuiti.[11] The condition caused the fleece to break off, leaving the sheep almost bare, and left ewes unable to feed and rear their lambs. Similar symptoms had been observed in sheep in Morton Mains in Southland, Glenhope in Nelson and in a district near Rotorua. DSIR scientists suspected that a mineral deficiency might be the cause. Dr R.R. Milligan and Professor John Malcolm had recommended Muriel as a suitable researcher.

Marsden appealed to Muriel on the grounds that the project offered 'the only means in New Zealand of carrying out the full tests which may throw light on the subject', and observed that the problem was 'of extreme, vital importance to New Zealand at the present time, as such a large area of land is "going back" merely because it has become "sick" in the above-mentioned sense'.[12] The problem thus was not simply a veterinary puzzle but also had implications for land settlement and New Zealand's pastoral economy. He asked her to investigate whether the illness was due to a calcium deficiency. Muriel accepted, finding the appeal to serve the national good difficult to refuse. 'Moreover,' she stated, 'the problem is one that interests me from the physiological aspect.'[13]

In an improvised laboratory consisting of a room with a water tap and an electric point, and with the sheep an hour's drive away, Muriel set to work to find out what was causing the disease. 'I did much more than calcium estimations, and I compared [the sheep under study] with sheep with bush-sickness. I found they were the same ... Sick sheep would recover if they were given a drench of iron and ammonium citrate. But I thought to myself as I saw them drink the large drench, what else does it contain besides iron? Some contaminating metal?[14]

The situation at Te Kuiti was baffling at first. A farm only a short distance away had healthy livestock, and '"a better farmer" was the hasty but erroneous judgment of neighbours who were similarly free from the trouble'. While Muriel was testing the sheep, Dr J.K. Dixon (a soil chemist) and Mr N.H. Taylor were surveying the area, not far from a series of cones of extinct volcanoes. 'The geologist remarked one day that the showers from past volcanic activity had left a sharp dividing line with different characteristics in fields that were in juxtaposition.' The answer did not come immediately, but 'some clues were obtained which later led us to try cobalt as a remedy and it worked wonders for the farmer'.[15]

In spite of Muriel's success in identifying a mineral deficiency as the cause of the illness, the primitive conditions in which she was researching and the limited time spent on the research meant that her efforts produced 'nothing worth publishing'.[16] There was a positive outcome, however, in that the DSIR decided to set up a nutrition laboratory for the agricultural industry (eight years before the establishment of any comparable institution for human nutrition).[17]

In other circumstances, Muriel might have been highly celebrated for this contribution to the New Zealand economy, but in the New Zealand of the late 1920s her patience, resourcefulness, perseverance and expertise went largely unrecognised. Her scholarship to London was awaiting her, and she left New Zealand with Jim Saunders on 7 December 1929, arriving in London in the middle of January 1930. Yet the Te Kuiti project could be said to have directed Muriel toward a topic of central importance in her life's work: the study of trace minerals and their effect on human health. Once in England, Muriel 'kept a watch on all the trace element work, by reading the journals as they came out in the library of the Royal Society of Medicine in London'.[18] In 1933 she thought she had a clue as to the type of mineral deficiency underlying bush-sickness in sheep, but the effect of the Depression in New Zealand meant that such research was put on hold.[19]

Return to England

Muriel's training in biochemistry in London was the cornerstone of her future career in nutrition. Biochemistry complemented her expertise in physiology, introducing her to new concepts and experimental techniques. The rapid expansion of physiology research in the 1920s occurred primarily in emerging fields such as endocrinology and nutrition: discoveries about hormones and vitamins lay within the purview of these new disciplines and were no longer considered part of traditional physiology. The most significant advances in the understanding of nutrition were being made in biochemistry. Complementing the understanding of the role of vitamins in human physiology, techniques for the synthesis of vitamins made it possible to treat diseases caused by acute vitamin deficiency.

If biochemistry was essential to the progress of nutritional science, advances in nutrition were equally important to the rise in status of biochemistry. Because of the widespread poverty and malnourishment caused by the Depression, the effect of poor nutrition on health brought the biochemical study of foods to international attention.

Progressive public policy in the 1920s and 1930s sought to apply scientific discoveries for the betterment of society and public health. Increasingly, governments were sponsoring scientific research to address social problems, and laboratory findings were being applied to public health work. At the same time, the trade union and labour movements were campaigning to make health a human right. Researchers were conscious of the links between poverty, poor nutrition and ill health, a relationship highlighted by the League of Nations Health Organisation during the 1930s.

Muriel started working at the Biochemistry Department at University College under Jack Drummond in February 1930. Drummond had graduated with a first-class degree in chemistry from King's College, London, in 1912 and became director of the Research Institute of the London Cancer Hospital in 1918. He took on the position of chair of the new department of biochemistry at University College in 1922, a role he held until 1945. His research with Katharine Coward on vitamin A from 1920 to 1925 was the foundation for much of the study of this fat-soluble vitamin in foodstuffs and pharmaceutical preparations such as cod-liver oil. Drummond's interest in practical and safe ways to remedy vitamin D deficiency led him to investigate the processing of cod-liver oil in the Norwegian fishing industry. In addition, he carried out research on the relationship of vitamin D to rickets and growth, and on sources of protein and vitamin B-1 (thiamine, then known as antineuritic compound).

Drummond became increasingly concerned with ways of providing adequate nutrition to low-income populations, especially during the Depression years. As his reputation grew, he lectured in the United States in 1933 and led investigations into nutrition in northern and eastern Europe in 1936. Although less polemical than Sir John Boyd Orr, the author of *Food, Health and Income*, Drummond helped to bring the problem of malnutrition among the working classes to the attention of politicians.[20] He had a long-standing connection to the People's League of Health, a British organisation founded in 1917 by former actress Olga Nethersole, which promoted nutritional education.

Drummond's interest in the history as well as the science of nutrition resulted in his book *The Englishman's Food*. Conscious of the detrimental effect of modern industrial processing on the nutritional content of foods, he pointed to the fact that eighteenth-century English peasants (who subsisted largely on soup, bread and cheese) had a better diet than the working classes of the twentieth century. Drummond went on to become an advisor on nutrition to the Ministry of Health, the British Medical Association and the League of Nations Health Organisation. As scientific advisor to the Ministry of Food during World War II, he tackled the challenges of meeting the nutritional needs of a nation at war.

Drummond's enthusiasm soon transformed University College's Biochemistry Department into a leading centre of biochemistry and biochemical research, attracting researchers from many countries. Another New Zealand graduate who worked there, Alice M. Copping, commented that 'the international exchange of ideas was one of the most valuable aspects of research in the Department of Biochemistry'.[21] Drummond and his wife happily received biochemists, overseas students and visitors in their home at Chorleywood, Hertfordshire.

Despite the attractions of Drummond's international profile and social concerns, his attitude toward women scientists in his laboratory was a potential barrier for Muriel. When Elizabeth Gregory, a home science graduate from Otago University, arrived as a research student at the Biochemistry Department in August 1929, she was apparently unaware that Drummond had banned all women from his laboratory. Her friend Elizabeth McLaughlin recalled, 'Into this somewhat chaotic and resentful situation firmly arrived "E. Gregory", certainly from New Zealand but startlingly not MR Gregory (in all correspondence that had passed she had never written her name in full. It was then, as for years, "E. Gregory"). Dr Drummond, expecting his embargo to be well known, had never thought to delve deeper.'[22] It is not known why Drummond capitulated or how long the ban lasted, but Elizabeth Gregory was allowed to remain and completed her PhD, 'without creating wild havoc in Dr Drummond's lab'.[23] It seems dubious that Drummond would have failed to infer Gregory's gender from her home science degree, but her account certainly makes for an entertaining tale.

Notwithstanding Drummond's official antipathy to women, three women from New Zealand – all Otago graduates – studied in his Biochemistry Department in the late 1920s and early 1930s. As a result, Drummond exerted considerable influence on New Zealand nutritional science.[24] Muriel Bell and Elizabeth Gregory returned to New Zealand. Alice Copping worked with Harriette Chick at the Lister Institute and then remained in England at King's College for Women.

Muriel studied in Drummond's laboratory for three years, from 1930 until 1932. She did not work toward a PhD, preferring to gain broad experience in a variety of experimental methods and techniques.[25] On Drummond's advice, she began by investigating the relationship of carnosine, a compound extracted from muscle, to the B vitamins, but abandoned the project after four months of fruitless work. She then turned to the study of vitamin A. The potential toxicity of this vitamin was of concern because it is present in high levels in fish-liver oils, which were recommended as a remedy for vitamin D deficiency. Experimenting on rats, she studied the toxicity of cod-liver oil, concentrate of vitamin A, and carotene. After four months of experiments, no toxic effects were evident, and she repeated the experiments using a higher dosage. Drummond suggested further work on the toxic effect of too much cystine in the diet and on pathological changes in animals with a vitamin B deficiency in relation to blood sugar and water levels.[26]

While based at University College Muriel took advantage of the free lecture courses available to her.[27] These apparently included a course of lectures in therapeutic dietetics. Covering the treatment of conditions such as diabetes mellitus, diseases of the alimentary tract, renal disease and hypertension, obesity, 'misc conditions', infancy and surgical conditions, the course focused on two main branches within nutrition: vitamins and food composition.[28] This interest was an enduring one: after her retirement in 1964, Muriel edited *Dietitian Tells Diabetic,* an advice booklet for people with diabetes and those who prepared food for them. It contained a basic summary of the dietetic principles of treating diabetes, followed by recipes and examples of food exchanges. Its resemblance to *Good Nutrition,* the government-sponsored nutrition and cookery book that Muriel later helped to produce, reveals the influence of Muriel's editorial pen and her confidence in the value of cookbooks in nutritional education.

In the 1930s some research in medical science was taking on a political slant. The enthusiasm for 'social hygiene' and its allied cause, the eugenics movement, may have left Muriel feeling ambivalent. She was never an active supporter or member of eugenicist organisations, such as the Sunlight League, but because issues such as venereal disease and birth control were of particular interest to medical women, she would have been brought into contact with these debates. As representative of the NZMWA, Muriel Bell attended the Fifth Imperial Social Hygiene Congress on 'The Venereal Diseases Problem throughout the Empire', organised by the British Social Hygiene Council and held in London in July 1931.[29] During sessions on the administrative measures and powers of government, the New Zealand Health Department warranted special mention for its wide powers, 'being authorised to order to hospital any infected person, and to institute legal proceedings against any who failed to take proper precautions against the spread of his infection'.[30]

To complete her research in London, Muriel requested an extension of her research scholarship for a third year in 1931. At the meeting of the Royal Society scholarship committee on 2 February 1931, the committee noted that letters of support had been received from Mr C.H. Fagge, vice-president of the Royal College of Surgeons of England and treasurer of the Royal Society of Medicine; Sir Ewen Maclean; and Mrs Chalmers Watson (Dr Mona Chalmers Watson). Lady Florence Barrett, former president of the MWIA, had telephoned in support of Muriel's application. These endorsements demonstrate that Muriel had managed to impress a number of distinguished figures in British medicine, particularly in obstetrics and gynaecology. Fagge wrote, 'I feel quite strongly that we have hit upon quite unwittingly as our present holder, an exceptional woman with the very rare instinct of the true researcher. The Committee will probably realise, as did I, when I learnt something of the question in New Zealand, that her work on nutrition of sheep was really of the greatest possible value.'[31] The committee granted the extension, and Muriel vindicated their decision in 1933 by publishing four articles in distinguished scientific journals: *Zeitschrift für Vitaminforschung*, the *Journal of Physiology* and the *Biochemical Journal*.[32]

Studying in London placed Muriel at the centre of international scientific discovery and brought her into contact with many prominent scientists. The Biochemical Society and the Physiological Society held scientific meetings a number of times each year. In June 1931, London hosted a Vitamin Congress attended by representatives from Europe and America. That September, the centenary meeting of the British Association for the Advancement of Science was also held in London, with one day of the chemistry section's meeting devoted to the chemistry of vitamins and related substances.

Muriel attended a dinner for New Zealand university graduates in London in 1933. Seated at the top table alongside John Malcolm and the New Zealand-born physicist Sir Ernest Rutherford, she wore an elegant evening dress. The photograph from this event is one of the few that challenge her reputation as a woman who did not care about appearances. During the evening she became involved in a conversation about university education in New Zealand. Rutherford, who, like Muriel, came from Nelson, argued that a population of one and a half million warranted there being only one university. Muriel disagreed but uncomfortably suppressed her own views.

Apart from her attendance at this event and her research collaboration with Elizabeth Gregory, the extent of Muriel's ties with other expatriate New Zealander students and researchers is unclear. As a married woman she was unable to take advantage of the opportunity to meet university women from abroad by living at Crosby Hall. One New Zealander noted that Muriel did keep in touch with Charles Burns, who had 'a nostalgic memory of a certain Sunday afternoon when a mutual friend of ours Dr "Onk" Williams and I went for tea with Muriel and her husband in their London flat'.[33]

During their years in London Muriel and Jim lived in private flats, first in All Souls' Avenue, Harlesden, and then in Hunter Street, near Russell Square in Bloomsbury. Jim took care of domestic chores while pursuing his political interests as a pacifist and possibly a communist. A 1938 article about Muriel in *Woman Today* sheds some light on their political involvement in London. 'While in London, she and her husband, who was especially interested in movements for peace and in assisting refugees from Germany, took every opportunity of hearing speakers on these and other allied problems, and made many interesting contacts with people who are leaders in progressive political movements. What time she could, Dr Bell also gave to her special interests, music and art.'[34]

It is difficult to know who these progressive leaders were, as Muriel's personal and scientific papers contain very few details of her years abroad. Certainly living in London offered ample opportunity to attend talks and lectures by prominent left-wing thinkers and leaders, and many scientists had ties to the Left.[35] There were like-minded scientists at the Dunn Biochemistry Institute, Cambridge, under Frederick Gowland Hopkins during the 1930s, a respectable minority of whom were women and married to co-workers at the Dunn.[36]

One small but intriguing piece of evidence of Muriel and Jim's political activity is a postcard sent by Jim from Berlin to Muriel at their Hunter St address around 1932. 'Have seen other partners of the firm but business is not good everything is very quiet. The old game of hide & seek is all the go here (among adults) but I am getting some business done. Remember me to Enfield and any others. Jim.'[37] As Jim was hardly a businessman, this presumably refers to some form of political activity in Hitler's Germany. The Enfield mentioned was most likely Alice Honora Enfield, the honorary secretary of the International Women's Co-operative Guild. This organisation focused on cooperative education and policy and lobbied for reforms to benefit married working women, such as a minimum wage and a maternity benefit.[38] In the 1930s the guild turned its attention to peace campaigning; it ran a dramatically effective campaign in 1932 using white poppies as an inversion of the armistice symbol of the red poppy.[39]

Training in British teaching hospitals, 1933–35

As the term of her scholarship neared its end, Muriel became anxious about her future. Arini Fisher (née Pope), her friend from Otago Medical School, wrote to John Malcolm: 'Muriel seems perfectly happy in her research work but I can't think what they are going to do when her scholarship comes to an end. She is worried about it too I know, but she will not even consider possibilities yet.'[40] Going home seemed to offer limited prospects: New Zealand was in the grip of economic depression, and Muriel later recalled that there were many New Zealanders seeking employment in London.

Moving on from University College, Muriel found employment at the Elizabeth Garrett Anderson Hospital (EGAH) as assistant pathologist under Dr E.H. Lepper. In this capacity she would have been involved in performing autopsies, examinations of organs and tissues removed during surgery, and routine laboratory tests. Dr Lucy Wills, with whom Muriel later travelled to Fiji on a medical expedition, had been appointed part-time biochemist in the Chemical Pathology Department in 1928. 'I worked for a year at the EGAH, along with the women physicians and women surgeons who ran it – it is run entirely by women – and they make a good job of it too.'[41] In 1934 Muriel worked at the Royal Infirmary Sunderland, again as assistant pathologist.[42] She learned, among other things, that New Zealand was well ahead of Britain in the prevention and treatment of diphtheria: here she 'came across more cases daily than she had seen in New Zealand'.[43]

In the north of England, Muriel saw the Depression at its worst. In coal-mining areas such as Durham and Northumberland, unemployment rates were frequently between 20 and 50 per cent.[44] Poverty and hunger were endemic. As attention turned to relief and welfare schemes, debates about food and nutrition became highly politicised. Studies showed that many families in the 1930s subsisted on poor diets, especially those with young children. In 1934 John Boyd Orr estimated that nearly 20 per cent of the population (about 10 million people) was living near or below the threshold of adequate nutrition.[45] Although some attributed these poor conditions to bad household management, another researcher, A.M.N.

Pringle, claimed that it was lack of money that caused nutritional problems in families.[46]

Muriel did not witness the 'disturbances' in New Zealand during these years, such as relief workers demonstrating against the unemployment crisis.[47] Her experiences in Britain, however, left a deep impression: 'Anyone who, like myself, saw something of mining towns in England and Wales during the depression, and beheld the grocers' shops with displays, not of New Zealand butter, but of all grades of margarine (then non-vitaminised) … felt alike an ache for the New Zealand farmer unable at that time to sell his butter, and for the miner who needed the vitamin A to prevent the industrial eye disease of nystagmus.'[48]

These experiences fed Muriel's belief in the possibilities of international cooperation to prevent disease and at the same time help the New Zealand economy. Rational organisation and scientific planning offered solutions to inequitable and inefficient systems of food distribution that contributed to malnutrition. In his history of the 1930s Depression in New Zealand, Tony Simpson remembers that 'generally people had an absolutely impossible diet'. Fresh fruit and vegetables were not available in the towns and cities, even though 'it was falling down off the trees by the hundreds of tons'.[49] He writes that people became accustomed to the lack of fresh foods, and it took some time for the health problems caused by poor nutrition to be recognised and dealt with. Malcolm McKinnon's history of the Depression records the all-encompassing nature of shortages in the early 1930s, extending even to the manure and seeds necessary for cultivating garden plots.[50]

Although the main problems lay in food distribution rather than outright shortages, malnutrition was still an issue. At the peak of unemployment during the Depression, malnutrition among New Zealand schoolchildren was close to 6 per cent; in 1932 school medical officers reported 'especially during the examination of city schools, increased evidence of the clinical signs of subnormal nutrition. The children were too pale, lacking in muscular tone and in general vitality … attributable to widespread unemployment.'[51] Schools established special classes for malnourished children, paying particular attention to nutrition, rest and outdoor physical activity. Annual health camps also benefited 'delicate and undernourished' children.[52] A scheme to provide milk in schools was proposed by the director of school hygiene, Dr Ada Paterson, as early as 1934.[53]

Muriel's years in Britain in the late 1920s and early 1930s could well have led to her settling permanently overseas; after all, the intellectual landscape in Britain was accommodating of Muriel and Jim's pacifism and left-wing views, and New Zealand still offered only limited opportunities for scientists to distinguish themselves. But political changes in New Zealand seemed to promise new opportunities for research and practice in public health. As part of its campaign, the New Zealand Labour Party planned to introduce a national health service.[54] The ensuing challenge of devising practical solutions to problems in food production and supply would allow Muriel to play to her strengths.

Chapter Five

GAINING GROUND IN NEW ZEALAND AFTER THE DEPRESSION

Muriel did not initially intend to return to New Zealand after her studies and work in London. According to a family member, the minister of health and education in the 1935 Labour government, Peter Fraser, may have been involved in convincing her to return home.[1] He had been instrumental in luring home other educated women, such as the radical feminist and socialist author Jean Devanney, with offers of important positions in the new Labour government. It is difficult to say what professional opportunities Muriel might have been forfeiting with this decision. Hospital positions in Britain were competitive, and her consecutive short-term contracts in clinical pathology departments did not offer much financial stability. While she seemed content with hospital laboratory work, paid research work would have made better use of her training in both physiology and biochemistry.

It is likely, then, that whatever opportunities Muriel was passing up in London, she hoped to find other rewarding challenges awaiting her in New Zealand. Initially, however, she must have felt a sense of déjà vu on her return, because she picked up almost exactly where she had left off five years earlier, resuming her position as lecturer in the Physiology Department at Otago Medical School. In 1936 she returned to her investigations into the problem of bush-sickness in sheep. Looking to the future, her most obvious career options were in teaching and applied fields, as pure research in New Zealand was still limited. (This limitation was not necessarily a professional barrier for Muriel: her practical solutions to problems like lack of staff and resources proved to be one of her greatest strengths.) But under a Labour government, welfare schemes were being established to remedy deficiencies of housing, health, education and employment. Its social security programme would offer access to free health care for all, and the government was also committed to expanding medical research, health education and preventive medicine. While Muriel had never had a strong interest in politics, Labour's vision, in particular the role of nutrition in improving the health of all New Zealanders, aligned closely with her personal views and professional expertise.

Scientific laboratory and social laboratory

While few written records document the relationship between Muriel and Labour Party cabinet members (telephone communication was more common), she was directly connected to politically active women. Peter Fraser's wife and assistant, Janet Fraser, was keenly interested in health, education, welfare and women's and children's issues, and in negotiating the relationship between politics and domestic life: according to one source, Janet 'saw the state as the home enlarged'.[2]

Labour policy greatly expanded the role of the state in people's lives. National health and housing schemes required a merging of private and state resources and resulted in policies that reached into the private home to improve public health. In the rhetoric of the Labour Party, the home was depicted as the foundation of the nation and the kitchen as the fuelling station of a nation of workers and growing children. The work of advisors such as Janet Fraser reflected the state's focus on the needs of women and families and the elimination of barriers between politics and domestic life.[3]

One example of this involvement arose from a dinner party to which Muriel had invited the Frasers and a member of Dunedin's Chinese community, Chin Bing Foon. The Bing family came from a village in China that was close to the Taishan railway, and Mrs Fraser wept when Mrs Bing told them how the villagers had crowded together to watch Japanese planes bomb the railway and had been bombed and machine-gunned in their turn. Janet Fraser said, 'Peter, we must do something to help these people.' The government's decision to allow Chinese war refugees to enter New Zealand may have had its roots in this social occasion.[4]

At the same time, Labour's agenda drew on scientific principles and rationales for advancing society and raising standards of living. In its project of bettering public health through improved nutrition, Labour had the support of international bodies such as the League of Nations Health Organisation. The New Zealand government was a signatory to the 1935 League of Nations declaration, which recognised that poor nutrition had become a widespread social and economic problem that was closely linked to world agricultural problems.[5] Peter Fraser's programme of preventive medicine placed special emphasis on public health education, improving infant welfare services, providing free milk in schools and better 'supervision' of Māori health.

With the 1938 Social Security Act, the government created a tax-funded health scheme.[6] Health was seen as 'an integral part of Labour's economic vision', which had been stimulated by the '"profound and pervasive" insecurity of the Depression'.[7] The financial viability of a government-funded health scheme in turn depended on disease prevention and health promotion, initiatives in which nutrition would play a vital role.[8] The state funded not only schemes for improving food distribution, such as providing milk in schools, but also nutritional research. Muriel's support for Labour's social welfare schemes set her apart from most of her colleagues in the medical profession, who resisted the idea of government intervention in their area of expertise.

When Muriel returned from London to the Physiology Department at Otago Medical School to work under John Malcolm in 1935, it was to resume a lecturer position for which she was overqualified and apparently required 'some pressure' to accept.[9] Malcolm had had constant problems finding skilled senior assistants in physiology, and Gordon Bell and Charles Hercus record 'the great indebtedness of the department to Dr Muriel Bell who more than once came to the rescue'.[10] Dr Murray Drennan reported to the University Council that it was 'very difficult to get the younger physiologists to go so far from the centre of things physiological, as they feared that they would thus be out of the running from posts in Great Britain'.[11]

However reluctant she may have been to return to this role, her students remembered the infinite care she took to produce 'beautifully scientific demonstrations' in the physiology and pharmacology laboratories. Her lectures were highly informative, and the concepts she taught proved valid in practice, much to her students' appreciation.[12] According to a tribute in the Otago Medical School *Digest* of 1940,

> Her serene influence over the practical physiology classes has been our inspiration for the last five years. We have always found her so incredibly cool and capable in the midst of rabbits and frogs – and those beastly little tin levers; she has always been sympathetic to our abandoned struggles with sooty bits of wire which can behave under examination stress in the most unreasonable and provoking manner. Most of us will remember her too for those wildly successful pharmacology demonstrations, which entailed an enormous amount of preparation and were so often received with riotous delight.[13]

For the most part, nutrition had received scant attention in the medical school curriculum. It was regarded as a form of complementary medicine at best, with much contradictory evidence coming from different researchers. As a lecturer in physiology, Muriel advised senior medical students on thesis topics, and by this method was able, to a degree, to incorporate nutrition into medical education.

Cobalt deficiency and bush-sickness

In addition to teaching, Muriel returned to practical research into cobalt deficiency. In 1936–37 she made four short visits to Morton Mains in Southland, where the sickness of sheep was causing considerable concern. In Malcolm's correspondence with Sandys Wünsch, then director of the Dairy Products company in Edendale, to arrange Muriel's visits, Wünsch noted that 'evidence for Co. [cobalt] deficiency being the root of the trouble seems very strong' and observed that another researcher was trying cobalt licks as a remedy.[14] On Blackmore's farm, Muriel tested animals' blood, liver and urine functions and found the same symptoms and biochemistry that she had found at Te Kuiti. Her colleague, the soil scientist J.K. Dixon, asked her for advice. Based on her knowledge of recent experiments by Dr Fred Stare, working in Wisconsin with Dr Conrad Elvehjem on rat nutrition, she suggested trying cobalt.[15] Dixon confessed in a letter, 'At the moment we don't know where to look for cobalt in the animal nor what a normal figure should be.'[16]

Muriel became further involved with cobalt investigations when Dixon was called back to his usual work on the soil survey, producing soil maps of the nation to aid in agricultural and horticultural planning. A major breakthrough in the sheep sickness problem came with the publication of an article by J.F. Underwood and E.J. Filmer, two Australian scientists who recorded their experiments on dosing sheep with cobalt.[17] Muriel's simultaneous work, although unpublished at the time, underscores her talent for research in challenging circumstances. In November 1936 Underwood visited Nelson and informed Dixon that New Zealanders appeared to be 'well up in the field, not only from the pasture top-dressing viewpoint but also from the analysis of sheep organs, since the Australians have been held up hitherto by the lack of suitable chemical method'.[18]

Muriel's expertise and interests were recognised with two important appointments. The first was as a member of the Board of Health, representing the interests of women and children, following the death of Lady Jacobina Luke in 1937. When Muriel was first appointed, the chief concerns of the board were water and sewerage problems, as deficiencies in public health were primarily associated with poor water quality, sanitation and hygiene. Muriel commented, 'You would be appalled to know of some of the affairs we have had to deal with.'[19] Looking back on her service toward the end of her term, she applauded the widened scope of 'public health' – including services for the deaf – under the remit of the Board of Health of the early 1960s. She held this position until her retirement in 1964.

The Board of Health appointment exemplified the professionalisation of women's unpaid role as guardians of health, both within the home and in voluntary and charitable capacities outside it. As E.R. Turner put it in a profile on Muriel for *Woman Today*, 'The present government is pursuing an enlightened policy in appointing women of such special [medical] training to commissions, councils, and boards on which their expert advice will be valuable.'[20] At the same time, a growing women's movement was calling attention to women's issues across the socioeconomic spectrum. Both progressive women's organisations and conservative maternal-welfare groups, often led by doctors' wives or middle-class professional women, were advocating for working-class women on issues like abortion and birth control.

In spite of her professional expertise, Muriel looked to ordinary women for ideas on how to address health issues facing women and children. Recognising the important role played by the Plunket system and the School Medical Service in improving the health of infants and school-age children, she perceived a gap in such services for children aged two to four. As a member of the advisory board of *Woman Today*, Muriel appealed to its readers: 'I should be glad to know if there were an expression of opinion in these columns as to the type of Welfare Centre, or other means, by which this need for the growing child might be met.'[21] A reader identifying herself as 'Moana', of Havelock, replied 'that the greatest problems of the kindergarten age call for psychological assistance', and suggested the expansion of existing education forums. 'I do feel most strongly that now the question of Public Health and the Birth-rate have become subjects of national importance, knowledge gained by modern research, together with the experiences of successful child-educationalists, should be made available to us young parents in the simplest and most inexpensive form possible.' Another reader predicted gloomily that the nation would 'jog along as of old – with much of the good that the Plunket Society has achieved for the baby – nullified by the treatment the child receives between two and five years old'.[22]

Despite Muriel's leftist politics and her commitment to women's health issues, it is problematic to label her views as feminist. On the one hand, she served as a role model to other professional women, seeming to defy what *Woman Today* called 'prejudice against occupation of public and professional positions by women … still prevalent in New Zealand'.[23] On the other hand, her approach aligns her more closely with welfare feminism, a philosophy popular among medical women in the interwar period. Unlike forms of feminism that primarily sought equality with men, welfare feminism focused on how the state could influence the well-being of women by improving conditions in the home, the chief site of women's labour. Muriel's awareness of and practical concern for affordable, healthy foods stemmed from both her gender and her working-class sympathies. In her view, women's primary roles as mothers and homemakers gave them significant social responsibility and the resulting power to determine the well-being of children and, by extension, the future of the nation.

Nevertheless, Muriel's concern with the political and social issues facing women was reflected in her public service in women's organisations as well as in her professional capacity at the Department of Health. An active member of women's organisations as a medical student at Otago University in the early 1920s, she returned to meet with her fellow alumnae and peers in the late 1930s. She was vice president of the Dunedin branch of the NZMWA in 1938–39, when the organisation grappled with questions about the civil, legal and political status of women and the admission of Jewish women into ancillary medical service.[24] Its actions to support refugee women in the years immediately before World War II dovetailed with initiatives by the New Zealand Federation of University Women to promote peace and provide financial aid to refugees. The federation made donations to the Women's Peace and Disarmament Committee. In addition, as head of the national executive of the NZFUW in 1937, Muriel put forward the motion 'that Home Science should cease to be compulsory in girls' schools, to allow the study of alternative science subjects, and that this meeting recommended the executive to forward this resolution to the Minister of Education [Peter Fraser]'.[25]

Her service on the advisory board of the feminist magazine *Woman Today* brought her into contact with other prominent women of her era, such as Robin Hyde, Sarah Page, E.F. Benson and Violet Hastings.[26] Muriel became a regular contributor to *Woman Today* on health issues such as hydatid disease (tapeworm infection) and foot care. She was also a founding member of the Dunedin Branch of the left-wing Progressive Publishing Society.

Toxicology of karaka berries

During Muriel's term of employment as a lecturer in the Physiology Department, she devoted her spare time to research work. One example was her investigations on the pharmacological aspects of hydatid disease; another was the toxicity of the karaka berry.[27] Dr Ada Paterson, the director of school hygiene, was concerned about the danger to schoolchildren of karaka trees growing on school properties and asked Muriel to investigate.[28] Māori used the berry as a food, but if not prepared correctly it was poisonous, capable of causing severe convulsions. Having read previous studies on toxic New Zealand plants by chemists at the Cawthron Institute, Thomas Hill Easterfield and Charles L. Carter, she began investigating the nature of the poison from a physiological point of view and searching for an antidote.

Muriel's experiments began in September 1937 with the effects of karakin, or hiptagenic acid, an alcoholic extract of green karaka berries, on a frog. She conducted additional experiments using rats, mice and rabbits. Muriel carefully noted the symptoms displayed, which often included increased respiration rates and convulsive movements. On the basis of the animal dosages, she calculated toxicity in humans, concluding that 8.4 grams of the extract would be lethal to a 70-kilogram human.

In March 1938 she began a new set of experiments with fresh batches of berries sent by friends and contacts from different parts of New Zealand. She ground the kernels of the berries, mixed them with a small amount of water and strained the liquid through a cheesecloth. This extract had no effect on a rat or guinea pig, but the equivalent of fourteen kernels was fatal to a cat.

In the next phase of the experiments Muriel focused on the berries' effects on pigeons. In her first experiment she recorded the effects of a dose of fourteen minced kernels: vomiting and regurgitation, 'a general impression of discomfort, and of weakness of legs and deeper slower respiration'. Within an hour and a half of force-feeding the pigeon, she observed a convulsion, which she compared to convulsions resulting from cyanide poisoning or vitamin B deficiency. One particularly resistant brown pigeon withstood the effects of twelve fresh berries made into a concentrate. The following day it looked 'alcoholic' and two days later appeared to be suffering from hallucinations, 'for it kept on pecking at the floor of the cage – when there was nothing there. Sometimes it seemed to imagine that the floor was water – made what appeared to be drinking movements'. It recovered within a week. Although she continued experimenting on kittens and pigeons, keeping careful note of the symptoms shown, her work on karakin diminished as wartime demands came to occupy her time, starting in 1939.

Her investigation into the toxicity of karaka berries in this period did not produce any conclusive results. She briefly returned to the problem in 1949 to test the effect of synthetic hiptagenic acid on pigeons and in 1953 to test the effect of an acetone extract of dried karaka berries in rats and pigeons, the latter proving highly lethal. Ironically, the subject was almost entirely neglected for the duration of her employment in the Department of Health. Only following her retirement in 1964 did Muriel return to address the toxicology of karakin with her characteristic scientific rigour.

Chapter Six

STATE NUTRITIONIST DURING WORLD WAR II

Muriel's appointment to the New Zealand Medical Research Council (NZMRC) in 1938 came with a more specialised remit than her Board of Health appointment. Established in 1937 under the leadership of the director general of health, the council consisted of two members of the faculty of medicine of the University of Otago, two representatives of the British Medical Association, two departmental officers, the director general of health and two members nominated by the minister of health, Peter Fraser. Charged with identifying the most pressing national health problems, the council set up committees on nutrition, thyroid disease and hydatid disease. Of these, nutrition research received the most funding: £800 per year. Fraser 'thought that what had been done in connection with the Council was the most advanced step ever taken in the Dominion in connection with the prevention of disease'.[1]

The Nutrition Research Committee

In some other countries nutrition research was largely the province of the agricultural sector and associated training institutions. In New Zealand it was led by the health and allied professions. The 1938 inaugural Nutrition Research Committee (NRC) of the NZMRC (also referred to as the Nutrition Committee) consisted of a formidable group of New Zealand's research elite: Professors John Malcolm, Charles Hercus and Elizabeth Gregory, Dr Michael Watt and Muriel.[2] As chair, Malcolm drew on forty years of experience in nutrition research. Muriel's great respect for and loyalty toward him were based on his dedication and high ethical standards. In this role, she later wrote, he contributed 'for a decade this highly-qualified though unpaid service work for the community … He refused to have anything to do with a monetary grant tagged with a condition which prevented freedom to state the scientific truth.'[3]

Charles Hercus, dean of the Otago Medical School, was a strong public health advocate. Since his appointment as professor of public health and bacteriology in 1921, Hercus had stressed the importance of social and preventive medicine, and he did important early work in surveying goitre among schoolchildren.[4] He also instituted a programme whereby students undertook research projects toward a public health thesis as part of the medical degree.

Elizabeth Gregory, Muriel's fellow postgraduate in the Biochemistry Department at University College in London, had become a lecturer in chemistry and nutrition at the University of Otago's School of Home Science on her return to New Zealand in 1931. She went on to become professor and dean of the School of Home Science in 1941.

Michael Watt was director general of health and chair of the NZMRC. Watt's distinguished career in public health administration began in 1920 as the first director of the newly reformed Division of Public Health. In 1930 he became director general of health, and the establishment of the NZMRC in 1937 was one of the major achievements of his directorship.[5] The year following its inception, the council established its 'main brain child', the Nutrition Research Committee, which oversaw the Nutrition Research Department (NRD).[6]

Muriel Bell was the beating heart of the Nutrition Research Department during its existence from 1938 to 1964. Her unique background, combining medical training, physiology, hospital pathology and nutrition research, shaped the work and profile of the department, which Charles Burns later described as 'the main target of [her] devotion'.[7]

The Physiology Department of the Otago Medical School was a natural place for the NZMRC to base the NRD, since both Bell and Malcolm were staff members. These links fostered collaboration with medical colleagues and provided training opportunities for nutrition researchers. The nearby School of Home Science proved a fruitful source of graduates for Muriel's research department. Master's degree recipients in home science were trained in biochemical techniques to a very high standard under Professor

Ann Strong and later Elizabeth Gregory. Bell's nutrition research workers played a key role in distinguishing nutrition research from other research departments. These combined attributes of the department fired Muriel's fierce loyalty to Dunedin as the home of nutrition research in New Zealand.

In addition, Otago Medical School had the advantage of being able to house research departments and thus avoid creating 'a medical research institute out of touch with medical education and future medical research workers'.[8] On his appointment as dean of the medical school in 1937, Hercus was immensely keen to foster internationally renowned research. While the school had a strong reputation as a centre for training general practitioners, its research had so far 'failed to attract attention because it was not very original or not very significant'.[9] There were exceptions, such as the neuroanatomy of the tuatara, the fieldwork on goitre and work on the pathology of the thyroid gland. The interconnectedness of Otago's research units and government departments reflected the common goal of improving public health.

Dietary surveys

One of the legacies of the Depression was poor nutrition, and national and international efforts to remedy the situation called for extensive dietary surveys. Previous statistics had relied on yearbook records of national food consumption, but closer inspection proved that these were often misleading. For example, the yearbooks showed that New Zealanders ate too much meat, sugar, cakes and confectionery and too little fish, raw fruit, raw vegetables, milk, eggs, unrefined cereals and cheese. Records of national consumption of foodstuffs alone, however, did not contain enough detail or analysis to shed light on potential deficiencies that resulted from the national consumption figures. As Muriel explained, 'We had to know not only what kind of foods, but how much of them [people] actually ate. This involved visiting homes, explaining how to keep records of foods purchased; foods were weighed before and after meals, so that we would know the amount trimmed from the food before cooking, and the amount of bone and scraps left on the plates.'[10] Through dietary surveys, women became creators of scientific knowledge, not simply consumers or educators.

By the beginning of 1939 researchers had completed dietary surveys of basic-wage earners in the tramway and boot and shoe industries in Auckland, Wellington and Christchurch. The researchers paid particular attention to the energy, protein, calcium, phosphorus and iron content of the diet and compared the results to standard dietary recommendations.

The most important discovery was the low intake of calcium, resulting from low consumption of milk and cheese and a preference for butter and cream, which were higher in fats than in milk solids. To increase calcium intake, the NRC recommended improvements in dairy production, government dairy subsidies and the establishment of town milk councils. This combined approach was necessary to make milk and cheese both affordable and popular and to make them a regular component of the New Zealand diet.

Another important nutritional defect that came to light in the surveys was iron deficiency, which was more common than expected among urban workers. Yearbook records had led to the assumption that the intake of meat, the main dietary source of iron, was high, but this was the case in rural areas only.

The dietary surveys provided a useful basis for future research, and justification for such schemes as milk in schools.[11] The studies also proved immensely valuable for determining the allocations of foods for rationing and for nutritional planning and education during World War II.

Keen to foster a positive relationship with the medical profession, the Nutrition Research Committee distributed a questionnaire to doctors about their patients' diets in 1939. It contained questions on the prenatal diet of expectant mothers, diet during lactation, infant feeding and the diet of pre-adolescent children. The department circulated the questionnaire to 700 doctors nationwide, of whom 47 per cent responded. While nutrition researchers did not anticipate that 'the answers would give adequate scientific basis for determining a clear line of future work … the questionnaire [was] valuable if only to get into touch with any who are keen to collaborate or who know of places where experiments have been or could be done'. Among the respondents, the issue of greatest concern was dental caries. Other concerns included goitre, rickets, gastric and duodenal ulcers, rheumatoid arthritis, constipation, diabetes and hypertension.[12]

In addition to work on calcium deficiency in children, the NRC's plans in 1939 included research into dietetic imbalances, such as the high consumption of butter; studies on vitamins A, B and C; diseases resulting from deficiencies of cobalt, fluoride, manganese, zinc and copper; projects comparing the nutritional status of children fed with the infant formula devised by the Truby King, the founder of Plunket, with other bottle-fed children; and joint work with the Goitre Committee on iodine metabolism.[13] The NRC always intended that experimental work on humans and animals would form an important part of its work, and to these ends 'the service of a trained physiologist, who had a thorough training as a biochemist and who had proved his ability to do research on nutrition would be necessary'.[14] Other lines of investigation included research on bread and flour, and dietary studies in farming and Māori areas. With the outbreak of World War II, however, the department narrowed its focus to the challenge of supplying the necessary intake of vitamins in the face of food shortages.

The school milk scheme

The introduction of milk in schools by the Health Department in 1936 signified a real advance in public health as well as a boost to the country's agricultural sector. Because the Depression had lowered the overseas price of dairy products, a scheme to offer every New Zealand schoolchild half a pint (300ml) of milk a day was of benefit to children and farmers alike. Initially, however, the scheme was not embraced by the dairy industry, whose interests had centred on securing prices and quotas of butter and cheese for export to Britain.[15] The idea that increasing the domestic consumption of milk could stabilise the industry found little resonance.

The scheme met with various other objections, accurately predicted by an advisor to the minister of finance, the economist W.B. Sutch: 'We shall be told that milk is a carrier of germs; that milk is not a perfect food; that it is not the business of the State to guarantee the minimum standards of physical existence; that it cannot be done in a big school; that secondary schools lads will either not require it, or will think that it is a food only for the very young; and probably the most basic reason will be advanced last – "that we don't like milk anyway".'[16] Sutch, like Muriel Bell and many others who had witnessed the widespread socioeconomic hardship of the Depression, looked to industry and trade to secure a stable economic future for New Zealanders. Some favoured a voluntary rather than nationally mandated scheme, asserting 'that it is neither seemly nor desirable to look to the State for every variety of assistance'.[17]

Although milk had not previously been seen as an important food for school-age children, a consensus on its benefits was growing. The League of Nations Technical Commission on Nutrition advocated an allowance of one litre of milk for a child or adolescent as sufficient for providing the protein, calcium and vitamins needed for growth. In a study that greatly impressed educational and nutritional authorities, Dr Harold Corry Mann, an employee of the British Medical Research Council, had reported in 1926 that a ration of milk promoted increased growth, vitality and liveliness in boys at a British boarding school.[18] Dental experts had previously believed that milk encouraged dental decay by leaving a film on teeth, but by the 1930s they had begun to focus instead on the ill effects of sugar on teeth and began extolling milk's virtues, including its effectiveness in forestalling a 'visit to the nearby sweet shop during recess'.[19]

The proposal had the support of various charitable and welfare organisations. School milk schemes were already operating on a local basis, one example being the New Zealand Smith Family Joyspreaders, which advocated milk in schools in Wellington as early as 1933. Its board consisted of powerful politicians: Minister of Finance George Forbes and Prime Minister Gordon Coates served as president and vice president in 1935. Health Department publications during the early 1930s promoted the importance of milk in bringing up 'healthy and virile' children.[20] The League of Health of New Zealand Youth and the Sunlight League campaigned vigorously for a national milk scheme for children.[21] The idea received a significant public boost when George Bernard Shaw, visiting New Zealand in 1934, suggested in a radio broadcast that milk could be supplied free to schoolchildren.[22]

The establishment of the scheme was, however, largely due to the findings of one north Canterbury high school teacher, H.C.D. Somerset. Noticing that his pupils often appeared fatigued, he published a report showing the need for improvement in children's diets. He ascribed the malnutrition that he observed not to poverty but to the lack of knowledge about the nutritional superiority of milk to cream and the importance of vegetables in the diet.[23] An early example of a dietary survey among New Zealand school children, it led the way for the kind of work later carried out by the Nutrition Research Department and brought the shortcomings of teenage children's diets to the attention of educational authorities.

New Zealand inaugurated its national school milk scheme in 1936. Schoolchildren received their first deliveries of milk in 1937. By 1940 daily milk delivery was available to 189,553 children, 67 per cent of all those in school. The following year more than 81 per cent of schoolchildren received milk daily; an educational journal noted that milk in schools had become an 'integral part of the school routine and teachers themselves know that the effect of this daily ration is a definite and in some cases substantial appreciation in the physical well-being of the children'.[24] In isolated areas where it was not possible to deliver fresh milk to schools each day, there were provisions for offering cocoa or alternative drinks containing malted milk powder.

Muriel's strong and enduring relationship with the dairy industry began with the school milk scheme. Her particular contribution to its success was to ensure that the milk contained maximum flavour and nutrients. Because the New Zealand dairy production until then had focused on supplying milk for commercial purposes, which did not necessarily meet the government standards of fitness for human consumption, making milk available to all schoolchildren nationwide was an onerous task. Standards of hygiene on farms and in processing required significant improvement, and safe and efficient methods of distributing milk to schools had to be devised.[25] The findings of a royal commission of inquiry into the supply of milk in towns in 1943 resulted in the formation of the Central Milk Council, which functioned as a government advisory body and promoted the production and distribution of safe, good-quality milk for all town districts. It also administered the milk in schools scheme until its abolition in 1967.

At the request of the minister of health, Arnold Nordmeyer, who was also chair of the Central Milk Council, Muriel joined the council as the representative for the interests of women and children. This was the third appointment she held in this special-interest capacity, in addition to her roles on the Board of Health and the Medical Research Council. Nordmeyer emphasised that the council's activities 'should reflect in a higher standard of health. They would, while not vitally interested in the economic side of the industry, have to make decisions which would possibly affect the economics of the industry and indeed the livelihood of some of those employed in the industry.'[26]

Muriel was initially reluctant to become a member of the council, 'knowing that there would be a great deal of work involved'.[27] Nevertheless, she served on the council for thirty years, until 1974. She chaired the Technical Subcommittee on Standards for Quality of Milk, which dealt with the production, handling and distribution of milk and the development and enforcement of quality standards. Elizabeth Gregory and Helen Deem, medical advisor to the Plunket Society, were also members of this subcommittee. According to Muriel, quality was the most important factor in changing attitudes toward and increasing consumption of milk. 'Unless we have milk matters right, we cannot achieve the dietary standards and adjustments that are part of a proper nutritional programme.'[28]

One important challenge was promoting pasteurisation, as tuberculosis was persistent in dairy herds. In 1944 the medical officer of health for Auckland recorded a 10 per cent rate of positive tuberculin tests in cattle.[29] Yet schoolteachers often blamed pasteurisation, rather than substandard hygiene and handling, for the poor taste of school milk and its unpopularity with schoolchildren. This low quality led to 'a vicious circle of low demand, low production, low quality and weekend surpluses'.[30]

The subcommittee recommended protecting milk from light to improve flavour and vitamin content.[31] Muriel explained: 'Light destroys the riboflavin content of milk and also has the effect of producing an unpleasant odour and taste ... Riboflavin gets transformed into lumiflavin which accelerates the destruction of the vitamin C in milk, and when the vitamin C goes, there is nothing to prevent the oxidation of the fatty acids from which therefore the milk develops a rancid taste.'[32] She confirmed these findings in a 1948 report showing that sunlight damaged the vitamin content of milk.[33]

These problems applied to both school and home milk deliveries. Milk wagons were exposed to the sun, milk was left on the doorstep or at the gate, and it was unclear whether coloured glass bottles had any effect in preventing deterioration.[34] The subcommittee recommended that milk should be delivered in sealed containers to prevent damage during transport, and that each local milk authority should set up a milk-testing laboratory.[35] In spite of the frustrations Muriel experienced in obtaining adequate quantities of milk and suitable testing facilities, by 1948 she was able to report 'definite progress … in laying the foundations for improvement in the quality of milk'.[36]

Encouraging the domestic consumption of milk also supported a national strategy to increase agricultural exports. In terms of yield per acre, dairy farming was a more efficient source of protein than meat production. Muriel was keenly aware of both the role that the export market played in New Zealand's economy and the possibility that New Zealand products could improve the health of people on the other side of the world. 'Much of our economic stability here in New Zealand depends on the things the people in other countries can buy.' When visiting mining villages in South Wales in 1930–34, she recalled, 'I used to think it would pain New Zealand to see the grocery shops full of margarine instead of butter.'[37] She advocated new ways of processing dairy products for export. For example, vast quantities of skim milk from butter making could be converted into milk powder for people who could not afford or obtain fresh milk. 'Now', declared Muriel, 'New Zealand will have to sit up and take notice of ideas like these.'[38]

Muriel used her scientific background to promote the sales of skim milk powder. In 1940, for example, she advised the Council of Organisations for Relief Services Overseas (Corso) against spending its annual funds on vitamin capsules for distribution in underdeveloped countries, and instead recommended providing powdered milk as a source of protein for infant feeding. Years later, Muriel noted the success of her approach:

> I had in mind that it would be good for New Zealand if at the same time as we were sending a source of protein for infant feeding, we were simultaneously building up an appreciation of milk as a food in countries which might then become purchasers of our milk powder. I think it is obvious that this has helped to expand our overseas markets in India and Asia. By meeting scientists from Africa while on my overseas sabbatical leave I have also been able to do some lobbying for the New Zealand milk powder trade … It is only by having a knowledge of overseas needs (a knowledge that stems from reading the scientific literature and having discussions among our research staff) that one can effect these rapprochements.[39]

In 1952 the Central Milk Council became the New Zealand Milk Board under the new Milk Act. Muriel accepted a nomination to the restructured board by Hilda Ross, the minister for women and children. Muriel assured Ross that 'progress will continue to be made in assuring our towns of milk supplies that are unimpeachable'. With respect to the elimination of bovine tuberculosis and the sale of raw milk, she stated, 'It worries me that we have not yet accomplished all that I had envisaged.'[40] The economic argument for culling tuberculous cows from New Zealand's dairy herd was compelling, she pointed out: the cost of paying compensation to farmers was far less than that of treating tuberculosis patients, which cost £1000 for a hospital bed per year. Muriel was often the one to give voice to reason where economic and health sectors intersected. She continued to work together with industry for the sake of consumers for forty years until the scheme ended in 1967.

Educating the public

The most urgent task facing the NRC was educating the public about nutrition. As Muriel recalled the situation, 'People were clamouring at the time for more information – and there were literally no posters or food models or pamphlets to help in teaching them.'[41] The New Zealand Women's Food Value League (NZWFVL) was formed in 1937 with the aim of spreading nutritional knowledge, fostering research and education on nutrition in general and undertaking research on local foods.[42] Its members included urban, educated middle-class women like Betty

Lorimer, Dorothea Turner, May Martin-Smith, Dr Violet Hastings, Wyn Good, Dr Barbara Roche and Agnes Loudon.[43]

Part of the challenge was to alleviate the confusion and frustration caused by the poor communication of scientific findings to the public. Guy Chapman, a laboratory researcher for the NZWFVL, commented of the housewife: 'Vitamins are haunting her dreams; she knows that her family may be starving on a full stomach; she realises that the basket of expensive food stuffs purchased on Friday for the week-end food supply may yet be essentially deficient in the necessary elements for building up healthy bodies and resisting disease.'[44]

Whether as dieticians, Plunket nurses, housewives, mothers, home science teachers or rural sociologists, women generally had the strongest personal and professional interest in nutrition. Professional publications and women's magazines were unanimous in declaring good nutrition to be a key element of a well-managed home. *Woman Today* was one such source of information. From its first publication in 1937, it regularly featured articles on diet and health. One editorial observed: 'Every woman with a family under her care is deeply concerned with public health. It is her duty to see that each member of the household is kept fit and well, and in carrying out that duty she is contributing to the welfare of the people as a whole.'[45] An agricultural journal similarly extolled 'the importance of prevention of sickness, the correct food for health, the living habits that promote health … The most important industry in New Zealand is the management of the New Zealand home!'[46]

A popular cookbook, *Whitcombe's Everyday Cookery*, stipulated that the housewife 'must have some knowledge of foods and the function each performs in nourishing the body, together with a knowledge of the energy requirement of each member of her family'. On top of these more scientific demands, the housewife was expected to provide varied and appealing meals. On account of its unnatural combination of flavours, 'A meal containing three foods such as salmon, tomatoes and prunes is an unpardonable error.'[47]

Some considered this task too onerous. An article in *The Nation's Larder and the Housewife's Part Therein* commented that in order for the housewife to balance the household diet scientifically,

> she would have to know and cater for many different daily needs of calories, of two types of proteins, of at least four inorganic substances – two metals and two non-metals – and of seven different vitamins. It is probable that no person, even those versed in dietetics, could carry in their heads the calorie values of the fifty or sixty different foods which we eat; their percentage compositions as regards first- and second-class proteins; the amounts of calcium, iron, iodine and phosphorus in those foods and the distribution of the various vitamins among them. It is therefore unwise for the housewife to attempt to do so and indeed unwise for her to trouble herself much, if at all, about calories, proteins, inorganic elements and vitamins.[48]

In collaboration with the NZMRC and Otago Medical School, the NRC attempted to address these difficulties by publishing a booklet outlining the principles of good nutrition, which first appeared in 1939. Simply titled *Good Nutrition*, it was intended to replace a 1935 Health Department publication, *Hints on Diet*. Elizabeth Gregory and Elizabeth McLaughlin (née Wilson) were the main contributors, Muriel was the editor, and John Malcolm contributed a chapter on the physiological principles of digestion.[49]

Good Nutrition was filled with recipes and weekly menus that included adequate amounts of milk, vegetables and fruit and offered alternatives to New Zealanders' traditionally high intake of meat, butter and sugar for families on a limited budget. The idea of a cookbook as a vehicle for basic nutritional education appealed to Muriel's practical nature: in response to John Boyd Orr's declaration that every housewife should possess a copy of the League of Nations booklet *The Physiological Basis of Nutrition*, she commented that she feared 'very few housewives would understand it'.[50] The first edition of 10,000 copies of *Good Nutrition* sold out, and it soon became the standard guide to nutrition in New Zealand. Nurses recommended its menus to patients, and pharmacists stocked copies for sale to customers interested in healthy eating.[51] Muriel remained its editor throughout its many subsequent editions and reprints.

Nutrition as an emerging science

To be effective, the Health Department needed to create a consensus on nutritional advice. But in the 1930s there existed divergent opinions on the benefits and harms of foods, and health advisors, like the general public, had difficulty in distinguishing sound scientific knowledge from 'nutritional quackery'.[52] Nutritional scientists were still struggling to establish their credibility and authority. One vocal opponent was a Whanganui doctor, Ulric Williams, who wrote to the prime minister criticising the NZMRC, as its members included 'several from the very fountain head of the enemies of truth!'[53] Williams had his own idiosyncratic views on nutrition and health: he stated in a public talk on infantile paralysis (poliomyelitis) that it was a deficiency disease similar to beriberi.[54] But even some of the more rational members of the medical establishment questioned the value of nutritional science. In a series of editorials on nutrition published in 1938, the *New Zealand Medical Journal* reported that the majority of doctors were dubious about the latest discoveries on vitamins. 'Side by side with the literature on the subject has risen a quasi-scientific and not disinterested propaganda which is promulgated to the general public – a body already morbidly conscious of its stomach. Thus are our patients rendered dangerously receptive to unproven and unjustifiable hypotheses in the sphere of dietetics.'[55]

The public health challenge of improving nutrition went beyond simply providing sound advice. It also required continuing laboratory research and intervention in industry practices, food storage, grocers' shops and the affordability of foods, not to mention household cooking habits and eating habits.

The complexity of the task may have been one reason that the Nutrition Research Department had trouble finding a candidate for the position of full-time research officer to the Nutrition Research Committee. Without such an officer to supervise the activities of the NRD, important work was being delayed. In the beginning Muriel Bell and Elizabeth Gregory were the only two members available to meet, and they frequently did so without calling an official meeting. Charles Hercus was given the task of recruiting suitable candidates while abroad in 1939, but it was often difficult to recruit experienced overseas scientists for New Zealand posts. Moreover, there remained some 'uncertainty about engaging anyone from outside NZ when we could not definitely offer security of tenure'.[56]

The committee's inability to recruit and appoint a research officer led to criticism of John Malcolm, the committee chair. In June 1939 Muriel wrote to Michael Watt, the director general of health, to express her concerns about Malcolm's well-being and the stress he was under in trying to carry out his NRC duties as well as those of professor of the Physiology Department. 'I know,' wrote Muriel, 'that he feels very worried and depressed.'[57]

Muriel considered applying for the post of nutrition research officer, writing to Watt, 'I cannot think of anyone in N.Z. who is likely to be suitable for it.' She had the training required in both physiology and biochemistry. The disadvantages to her taking on the post were a drop in salary and insecurity of tenure. 'But on the other hand,' she countered, 'I should find it interesting. And I did three years training in England along these lines.'[58] She mentioned an alternative arrangement suggested by Malcolm, that she take over as chair of the NRC and manage with Home Science graduates as nutrition research officers. 'But', she observed, 'that leaves Dr Malcolm's future rather dark. The affairs of the Physiology Dept are in the melting pot at present. They will soon want to know whether they should advertise my position as well as Edson's; and I feel that what I shall do will depend on whether you have any plans for Dr Malcolm's future or not.'

The NRC recommended the appointment of Muriel as nutrition research officer at a salary of £800. The committee sought to expand her work in collaboration with other research institutes, such as the Wheat Research Institute in Christchurch. Watt put the recommendation to the minister of health, Peter Fraser, before he left for England.[59] What emerged out of this correspondence was a proposal that Muriel take on the expanded role of nutrition research officer to the Health Department. Rather than working under the aegis of the Medical Research Council, she would report directly to the director general of health.

Initially, Muriel was 'staggered' by the range of tasks for which she would be responsible and feared 'that these would prevent any continuity in a research programme'.[60] Malcolm persuaded her to consider the offer, and she summarised her assessment of its advantages and disadvantages in a letter to Watt. The security of tenure made the Health Department post more attractive than the NZMRC appointment, which offered only a five-year term – 'a decided risk at my age', Muriel noted. But she had real concerns about the scope of the role. 'The more active part of your programme made me shrink,' she confessed, 'because having lived so long the life of a laboratory recluse, I doubted whether I should now be temperamentally suited to make the approaches that the school work would entail. On the other hand, such approaches will have to be made if there are dietetic investigations, whether it be among pakeha or maori, children or adults, and that too would come under the pure research post.'

Factors in favour of Muriel retaining her current university post were that she was due for a sabbatical year and that she wished to remain in Dunedin, with its growing scientific-research culture. Yet she could have seen little prospect of career advancement in academic medicine. Otago Medical School did not appoint its first woman lecturer, Mary (Molly) Marples, until 1946, and Muriel considered that appointment a great step forward for university women.

Although the need to appoint a nutrition research officer was growing increasingly urgent, the NRC declined to rush into an arrangement with the Health Department: because of 'the unsettled state of affairs brought about by the war, Dr Watt advised that the matter be left in abeyance until policies with regard to research were more definitely crystallised'.[61] The war had intensified with Germany's Blitzkrieg bombing of strategic English cities in May 1940. Peter Fraser, now prime minister, urged support for Britain in his 'Darkest Hour' speech: 'All that we have and all that we can do must be at the disposal of our cause, the cause of the Motherland, the cause of the Commonwealth.'[62]

Muriel's life was thrown into even greater turmoil when Jim Saunders died of a heart attack on 31 May 1940. In view of her strong pacifist beliefs and her respect for Jim's, it must have been difficult for her to decide to take a government post during wartime. It is even possible that this choice led to her falling out with staunch pacifists like Archibald and Millicent Baxter. But her desire to put all her efforts into serving the welfare of women and children apparently overrode any doubts about the morality of war.[63]

In October 1940 Muriel was made an officer of the Department of Health as state nutritionist, which involved both research and service duties. She retained this dual role until her retirement in 1964. In the public education aspect of her new duties, Muriel frequently returned to the tried-and-true format of an everyday cookbook like *Good Nutrition*, as it was a genre appropriate for both home and school.[64] By translating recommended nutritional intakes into practical meal plans, recipes and household practices, Muriel contributed to the public understanding of nutrition, bridging the gap between the laboratory and the kitchen.

Muriel also wrote and contributed to other Health Department pamphlets, some written for the general public and others for specialised audiences such as teachers and dental nurses, covering nutrition, dental hygiene, maternal and infant welfare and Māori health. She wrote *The Family's Food, Children's Meals* and *The School Lunch* as well as its subsequent edition, retitled *School Lunches*.[65] A sample lunch for Thursday consisted of sandwiches of cottage cheese and chives, a date and lemon-juice sandwich and celery (accompanied by salt in a twist of paper). She also wrote *Milk for the Child* and *Household and Institutional Milk Recipes* as part of a series of pamphlets promoting pasteurised milk as a drink at home and in schools.

Other pamphlets were more admonitory in their attempt to change New Zealand dietary habits. *You Must Balance Your Diet* and *Take Your Lunch Seriously* warned against eating large helpings of cakes and scones at morning and afternoon tea, skipping lunch and choosing unhealthy restaurant foods. *Don't Waste Your Vegetables* encouraged wartime economising, and *The Meat Ration is Adequate for Good Health* sought to ease concern about the nutritional shortcomings of the wartime diet.

The advent of national radio broadcasts created a new medium for health education, one that Muriel saw as important for reaching members of the public who were not habitual readers.[66] The popular *Radio Talks on Health* brought the Health Department's messages directly into homes and kitchens. The *Listener* magazine was originally available free of charge to all subscribers of the National Broadcasting Service. In addition to advertising radio programmes, it featured articles on a range of subjects, and Muriel became a regular contributor on health matters. The popularity of the *Listener* series turned Muriel Bell into a household name.

Muriel understood that in order to influence the dietary habits of the general public, she had to make her advice understandable and appealing. She had a particular talent for translating the latest medical findings into straightforward language and explaining their significance for everyday cooking. Because of the high quality of the scientific information Muriel presented, her articles were also valuable to home science and hygiene teachers as classroom texts.

Muriel's series of articles on vitamin C in the *Listener* illustrate her approach to nutrition education. The disruption of shipping in the Pacific after the bombing of Pearl Harbor had led to a shortage of oranges, and New Zealand was at risk of a national vitamin C deficiency. In late 1941 she prepared a series of articles on the nutritional importance and alternative sources of vitamin C. Her list of references points to her erudition and skill in synthesising information: 'In addition to various scientific statements of which I cannot remember the source, I have used *Biological Oxidations and Reductions* by Szent-Györgyi, *Annual Review of Biochemistry*, tables of the vitamin content of human and animal foods, an article in *J. Chemistry and Industry*, a conversation with Mr Keyes of the DSIR, a scientific article in the *Lancet*, a recipe book in the German language, some newspaper cuttings I have collected and several days' work by Miss Barbara Johns.'[67]

Ever one to encourage resourcefulness, Muriel encouraged mothers to make rosehip syrup and preserve blackcurrants.[68] Because rosehips contained the highest amounts of vitamin C, she enlisted the assistance of Plunket nurses in gathering wild rosehips in the Central Otago region, and rosehip syrup became her trademark home remedy.[69] A cartoon featured in the *Listener* in 1943 after an amusing letter from a reader about the difficulties of making rosehip syrup, which began: 'I do not like thee, Dr Bell – The reason why this tale will tell.' Muriel also drew attention to alternative local sources of vitamin C, such as New Zealand grapefruit, which many South Island residents were unacquainted with, and she promoted the cooking water for vegetables as being high in vitamins.[70] 'It would be a good thing if we had a slogan to the effect that you could tell from her beautiful complexion that she drinks her vegetable water!'[71]

Bread and flour

Improving the nutritional value of bread and flour was another wartime project of the NRD. One way to do this was to fortify flour with vitamin B-1, but this was a costly choice in a period of austerity. Another was to modify the process of refining white flour to include a higher proportion of the wheat grain, thus retaining more nutrients and resulting in a higher total yield of flour. In 1946, as a response to the global food shortage, the Council of the United Nations Relief and Rehabilitation Administration appealed to all countries to raise the extraction rate of flour to 80 per cent. This percentage was a higher target than planned in the experiments of the NRD and the Wheat Research Institute.[72] Nevertheless, within a few weeks New Zealand's flour mills had raised their extraction rate from 73 per cent to 80 per cent.[73]

In the trial phase of this switch, the amount of bran retained in the flour resulted in soggy bread.[74] Eager for the policy to succeed, the NRC warned the public to expect these characteristics in their bread, and by the late 1940s, bread made with the new higher-extraction flour had become popular, improving the vitamin B-1 intake for 'the muscular worker'.[75] Moreover, because higher yields of flour per acre reduced the wheat subsidy paid to farmers, the government saved an estimated £250,000 annually.[76] In one report, Muriel noted, 'One has to have an authoritative back stop or shelter when it comes to an argument between the trade and the Minister, and the trade has been vocal in wanting to copy slavishly what is done overseas.'[77]

Alongside her hectic research programme, Muriel found romance amid her investigations of fish-liver oils. In an encounter at the Sawyers Bay research station near Dunedin, Alfred Hefford, the director of fisheries research, fell in love with Muriel at first sight.[78] They were married by the Reverend Colin Scrimgeour ('Uncle Scrim'), a national radio personality, on 20 June 1942.

Alf Hefford was English-born and, like Jim Saunders, was eighteen years Muriel's senior. He had spent many years working on fisheries in India before moving with his family to New Zealand in the 1920s. He had seven children from his previous marriage to his wife, who had died in

1940. All were grown up except for his youngest son, Jim Hefford, who was twelve years old when Alf and Muriel met.

The couple lived apart for the first three years of their marriage because of their work commitments: Alf in Wellington and Muriel in Dunedin, but Muriel's frequent visits to Wellington for her Board of Health and Medical Research Council meetings meant that she saw him often. Muriel had a difficult relationship with her stepdaughters and did not form close bonds with the other Hefford children, although Jim had fond memories of biking around Dunedin and amusing himself at the medical school during summer holidays. The remainder of the year Jim spent at boarding school or with his father in Wellington. Jim's visits put Muriel's nutritional advice to the test in feeding a growing teenager in the face of wartime scarcities. Jim did not recall ever going hungry, remembering bacon, eggs, porridge and toast for breakfast.[79] After his retirement in 1945, Alf joined Muriel in St Clair, Dunedin, where he cooked meals and looked after the home, just as Jim Saunders had done during Muriel's first marriage.

Chapter Seven

DRIVING DIETARY CHANGES FORWARD

Food shortages and rationing persisted in much of the world for years after the end of World War II. Although her primary nutrition agenda remained local, Muriel also became interested in shaping a role for New Zealand in solving the world food crisis by becoming a significant food exporter. Despite shortages of labour, fertiliser and transport, New Zealand was far better off than many other countries – Great Britain in particular – in having an adequately nourished population. Muriel wrote, 'The present economic crisis in Britain has called for a greater effort to produce food, and indeed there is a general feeling that, small though our capacity may be, we should relieve her to whatever extent lies in our power of the necessity for dollar expenditure on food.'[1] Finding a balance between national and international nutritional needs was a recurring theme in the postwar period.

Postwar nutritional programme

Postwar world food shortages differed from those in wartime. The problem was no longer that of transporting and supplying foods but rather insufficient production, and an international shortage of animal protein led to concerns about undernutrition and malnutrition. Placing additional pressure on food supplies strained by wartime damage was the need to feed a growing global population. Governments and international agencies, including the newly established Food and Agriculture Organization and the World Health Organization, called on scientists to increase the productivity of agricultural land and to develop strains of crops that yielded more calories and protein.

One method of increasing the carrying capacity of pastures was the use of artificial fertilisers. In New Zealand, the application of fertilisers had been steadily increasing since the 1920s, reaching 700,000 tons of superphosphates and 1.25 million tons of lime annually by 1954.[2] Nutritionists and economists proposed the goal of doubling total agricultural production in fruit and vegetables and dairy products, the latter giving New Zealand a unique opportunity to create a supply of dried milk products to meet the increased global demand for animal protein.

Rationing continued in New Zealand after the war, partly because of continuing world food shortages and partly out of solidarity with those subsisting on meagre rations in Britain and Europe. The British minister of food, Sir Ben Smith, stated that Britain needed fats, meat and sugar, and noted that New Zealanders' ample consumption of butter was one area where they could make more 'extensive sacrifices'.[3] Women's magazines suggested ways of economising on rationed foods to support the 'More for Britain' campaign.[4] Muriel contributed articles supporting the relief effort by pointing out that prior to rationing, New Zealanders and Danes had the highest rates of sugar consumption in the world. She reminded readers that too much sugar in the diet could cause health problems such as obesity, diabetes and dental decay.[5]

The voluntary practice of sending food parcels to Britain continued after the war. Recommended foods ranged from tinned meat, cheese, honey, and puddings to dried foods and home baking.[6] Fats were in particular demand. The efforts of keen volunteers resulted in the Barling fat scheme, through which New Zealand sent hundreds of 40-pound (18kg) tins of 'finest quality fat' to Britain – fat that was otherwise 'being wasted on the farms and in the homes of Otago and Southland'.[7] The tins were accompanied by letters of gratitude and appreciation: 'New Zealanders feel the bonds of Empire very strongly and you folks in our Mother country were so good to our boys during both world wars that [we will do] anything we can to help to repay you all for your hospitality and kindness to our sons and brothers. We shall always be in your debt in spite of all we can do.'[8]

Despite New Zealanders' efforts to ameliorate international food shortages, closer to home there still remained room for improvement. New Zealand boasted the lowest infant mortality rate in the world, but measures promoting health were still a necessary part of the public health infrastructure. The lack of conspicuous cases of vitamin or mineral deficiencies meant that poor dietary habits were often overlooked. Muriel's Dunedin colleague Helen Deem drew attention to the contrast between public health campaigns and popular habits when she complained at the Auckland Provincial Plunket Society Conference that 'beautiful posters' in railway refreshment rooms 'urge the public to eat nutritious foods, yet the meals inside consist to a great extent of pies, white bread and strong tea.'[9] Similarly, Muriel berated those who ate poorly in spite of an adequate income: 'Too many calories, too frequent meals, too great a tendency to choose cakes, scones, sweets and ice-cream, cream and butter rather than milk … Watch them including cake for breakfast at the railway-station refreshment-rooms, or cakes and buns to go with their midday cup of tea in cafeterias!'[10]

Somewhat paradoxically, rationing in Britain led to a marked improvement in general public health. Fortified bread and margarine, vegetables grown in home Victory Gardens, improved distribution of milk and the replacement of meat with eggs and cheese all ensured that people from all classes received adequate vitamins and protein, known as the 'protective foods'. The shortage of sugar reduced the consumption of unhealthy sweets.[11] Likewise, public campaigns in New Zealand urged householders to grow their own vegetables and fruit and to keep hens, but nutrition education did not always have the desired effect. 'Even if people could afford a good diet', noted Muriel, 'the foods chosen were not always very wisely selected.'[12]

Newspaper headlines in 1949 reported on malnutrition and poor food habits, although the causes were debatable.[13] The director general of health, Harold Turbott, observed that in spite of a wartime campaign to improve dietary knowledge among New Zealanders, the complexity of substitute foods and a reduced supply and choice of foodstuffs posed a significant challenge to New Zealand mothers.[14] For example, local fruit canning did not take off sufficiently during the war to compensate for restrictions on importing canned pineapple, peaches and apricots. On the other hand, the expansion of the vegetable canning industry resulted in plentiful supplies of green peas, asparagus, baked beans and tomato purée.[15]

Another of Muriel's public health concerns was the composition of rations for pregnant and breastfeeding women. Mothers required extra protein and other nutrients during both pregnancy and lactation. To get their quota of vitamin B-1, mothers needed to consume two pints (1.2l) of milk and their full ration of meat and eggs daily. Too often, mothers sacrificed their own rations to feed fathers and the rest of the family – a practice Muriel considered 'a very serious tendency'.[16]

Water fluoridation

Muriel's work on water fluoridation in the postwar years built on her earlier research on vitamin and mineral deficiencies. New Zealand soils were known to be deficient in trace elements and minerals, including iodine, cobalt, fluoride and selenium. Even so, it took years for research to demonstrate the efficacy of fluoride in preventing dental caries.

Muriel first took an interest in the role of fluoride in dental health in 1925 while lecturing dentistry students in physiology. She was keen to explain the high incidence of dental caries: by the age of twenty, New Zealanders on average had twenty-two decayed, missing or filled teeth.[17] She noted, 'Many mothers write to me to say how disappointed they are when, in spite of all their care about giving their children the right foods, the youngster's teeth have decayed badly, and they want to know why.'[18] Doctors shared this concern, as did medical officers involved in examining military recruits to serve in World War II: 'Their verdict is that the skeletal physique of New Zealanders is extremely poor by contrast with the sunshine and the wealth and productiveness of the country we live in, and that among the age groups being examined at present only about 1 in 10 or 12 have not artificial dentures.'[19]

While it was widely accepted that poor dietary habits and the consumption of large amounts of sugar were bad for teeth, comparisons with other countries suggested that other factors might also be in play. For example, the weekly sugar consumption in America was comparable with the rate in New Zealand, but dental caries was not as prominent in the United States. Muriel mused, 'I begin to wonder whether there is some specific soil defect which is becoming more pronounced as the soil becomes depleted, or whether the known deficiencies in our diet (chiefly iodine, calcium, vitamin D, and vitamin B1) combine to produce these defects.'[20] After reading a paper showing that fluoride hardened the teeth of rats, she suspected a deficiency in fluoride might be a contributing factor.[21]

Muriel appears to have contemplated research into connections between fluoride and dental caries as early as 1941.[22] But by 1943 she regretted that she was 'still unable to report any progress with the larger problems that badly need research, e.g. my hopes of tackling the fluoride problem in relation to dental caries have not materialised'.[23] The difficulty of the technique for measuring fluoride levels prevented her from taking on the chemical work herself. She hired a chemist, Dr C.J. Wilkins, whose preliminary researches had shown extremely low levels of fluoride in the water supplies he examined. But Wilkins left in 1944 to take up a university post, and because of wartime staff shortages Muriel's efforts to find another qualified chemist to complete the work were unsuccessful.

Typically, Muriel devised an alternative approach. She had read a 1942 report showing that the experimental application of fluoride to teeth arrested and prevented dental caries in young children, and she encouraged the members of the School Dental Service to perform similar experiments. Meanwhile, Wilkins trained Marion Harrison, a home science graduate with an outstanding academic record (later Professor Marion Robinson), to take over the project. She too found that the water samples she tested were extremely low in fluoride. At the same time, the Dominion Laboratory of the Department of Scientific and Industrial Research carried out tests on potable water supplies. Harrison's preliminary analyses showed results similar to those of low-fluoride areas in the United States. In 1945 Grand Rapids, Michigan, became the first city in the United States to institute water fluoridation. The NRD made the first plea for trial fluoridation of water in New Zealand in the same year, but it took nearly a decade before any local councils agreed.

Harrison wrote her master of home science thesis on the fluoride content of New Zealand teeth and worked in the NRD from 1946 until 1948. Her research showed the amusing fact that tea was a major source of fluoride in the New Zealand diet.[24] Her work also included public education about fluoridation and distribution of fluoride solutions and tablets. The NRD attempted to retain her services by offering her a research fellowship, but she went on to study for a PhD at Cambridge under Robert Alexander McCance, professor of physiology, on a Science Travelling Scholarship.[27] Harrison remembered Muriel as 'marvellous, she really was. I had contact with her when I did my masters on fluoride. That was a very rich experience. That just opened up doors.'[26]

Harrison was one of a number of accomplished women scientists in the NRD. A writer for the *New Zealand Woman's Weekly*, Ola Rudman, praised Muriel's five assistants, all of whom had home science or science degrees. 'These are all young women, and it gives one a glow of satisfaction to feel that these members of our sex are making their contribution to the world's pool of knowledge of nutrition.'[27] However, the NRD had difficulty retaining home science staff, as women typically left employment when they married. Isobel Wilson left at the beginning of 1945 when her husband returned from overseas. Elizabeth C.G. McLaughlin (née Wilson), who had been on staff since 1938, resigned in December 1945, and Evelyn Moore left to become assistant nutrition advisor to the Australian government in Canberra.[28]

Postwar social dynamics also affected the staffing of the NRD. Many women left the workforce as returned servicemen moved back into civilian employment. At the NRD, these included Geoff Dunckley, Rex Malthus, whom Muriel regarded as a 'first-class practical worker', and Dr G.M. Richardson, who joined the department in 1948 to study the toxic constituents of food. Muriel noted that Richardson 'fill[ed] the need that we have long felt for an experienced biochemist'.[29]

Meanwhile, Muriel's career continued to soar. The fact that she had no children may have exempted her from conventional expectations. She was offered the position of chair of the Nutrition Research Committee and chief supervisor in charge of nutrition research in 1949 – after all, she had been acting unofficially in that capacity for some years. Malcolm nominated her for the position, stating, 'She is the heart and soul of the committee and I cannot think of anyone else who would satisfactorily fill the position.'[30] Her workload continued to increase, demanding overtime and working on holidays to meet tight deadlines.

As chair, Muriel envisaged an ambitious plan to expand the research programme of the Nutrition Research Committee, moving away from routine analyses of foods, which other departments could perform, and toward the clinical aspects of nutrition, such as investigating kidney disease, obesity, cancer, dental caries, anaemia, mental health and diseases caused by vitamin deficiencies.[31] Muriel warned: 'The study of nutrition is still in its infancy therefore our ideas should not be too static or rigid. Be it admitted that nutrition collects a lot of cranky ideas, sometimes we take a view which is too myopic.'[32] Despite difficulties in the research field, there were already indications that nutrition was losing its paramount position in the hierarchy of medical research fields. Muriel's plans for expansion relied on additional funding to secure new staff appointments and equipment upgrades. The Health Department, however, did not share her views. The Nutrition Research Committee's budget for 1948–49 was cut substantially, from the previous annual budget of £3304 to £2394.[33] The NZMRC proposed a further reduction the following year, to which Muriel grudgingly agreed. Difficulty in finding suitably trained assistants was the major reason behind these reductions, but Muriel recommended some flexibility in the budget should an appointment become possible later in the year. She continued: 'I hope therefore, that the present attitude of Treasury is only a temporary one, and that it does not mean that there is to be no further progress in the field of nutrition research in New Zealand, especially when there is considerable expansion permitted in research activities in other departments less concerned with human health.'[34]

Thomas and Eliza Bell, c. 1886.

Murchison Historical and Museum Society

Bell family, c. 1895. Left to right: Elsie, Eliza, Leslie, Francis, Thomas.

Murchison Historical and Museum Society

Above: Eliza Bell was fatally injured in this tram accident in Brooklyn, Wellington, on 3 May 1907.

Watt, T (Miss), fl 1978: Photographs of Wellington and Napier scenes. Ref: 1/2-080520-F. Alexander Turnbull Library, Wellington

Left: Muriel graduated with the medical degree of MBChB from the University of Otago in 1922.

Author's private collection

Muriel was the only woman in New Zealand to hold the research degree of Doctor of Medicine (MD) at the time of her graduation in 1926.
Author's private collection

A sheep with bush-sickness, Te Kuiti, 1929. Muriel wrote about this image: 'Here is a photograph of one of the ewes, taken just a little while after she began to recover after being transferred to an unaffected pasture. See how her wool has broken off, and think what it means in terms of this country's income from wool.' Author's private collection

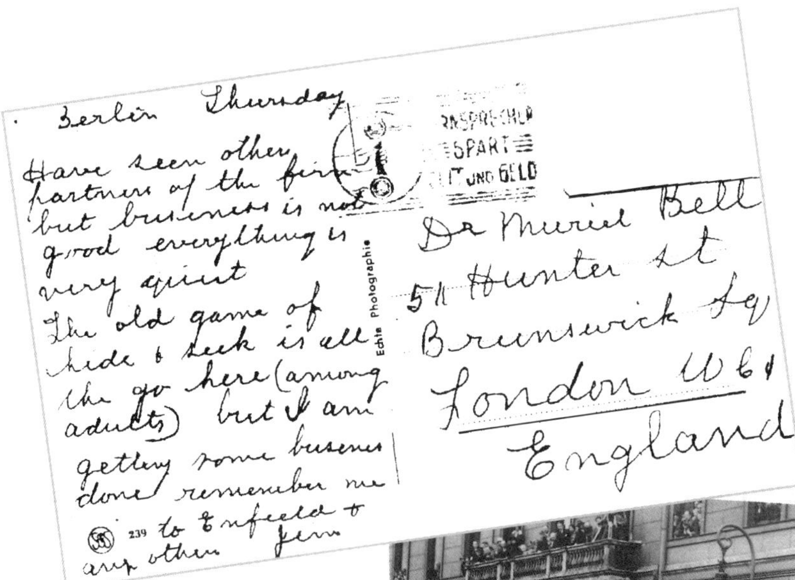

Berlin Thursday

Have seen other partners of the firm but business is not good everything is very quiet The old game of hide & seek is all the go here (among adults) but I am getting some business done remember me to Enfield & any other Jem

Dr Muriel Bell
51 Hunter St
Brunswick Sq
London WC1
England

Echte Photographie

239

A dinner of New Zealand university graduates in London, featuring Sir Ernest Rutherford, Professor John Malcolm and Dr Muriel Bell at the top table, c. 1933. Author's private collection

Jim and Muriel at their home, St Clair, Dunedin, 1938.

Author's private collection

Opposite: Jim sent this postcard from Berlin to Muriel at their home address in Russell Square, London, in 1932. The stamp has been removed by a collector.

Author's private collection

Above: Jim and Muriel at their home, St Clair, Dunedin, 1938.

Author's private collection

Left: This group features Jim and Muriel on the right, 1938.

Author's private collection

Muriel on her appointment as nutritionist to the Department of Health, 1940.
New Zealand Free Lance: Photographic prints and negatives, Ref: PAColl-6388-52, Alexander Turnbull Library, Wellington

This cartoon about Muriel's recipe for rosehip syrup featured in the *New Zealand Listener* in 1943.

NZ Listener, 30 April 1943, NZ & Pacific Collection, Ref: S-L-1319-9, Alexander Turnbull Library, Wellington

The front cover of the wartime edition of *Good Nutrition* (1944). It was reprinted in 1945.

Author's private collection

Opposite: Muriel using a microscope in the lab.

S14-589c Photograph of Muriel Bell, Margaret Madill papers, r.6653, Hocken Collections Uare Taoka o Hakena, University of Otago

Muriel adjusts the Soxhlet fat extraction apparatus used in research on the vitamin D content of fish-liver oil and butter, 1949.

Dr Muriel Emma Bell, 1949, Prime Minister's Department photograph, Box-184-127, Hocken Collections Uare Taoka o Hakena, University of Otago

Above and opposite: Muriel received an honorary Doctorate of Science from the University of Otago in 1968. Author's private collection

Otago Medical School researchers at the Purves Symposium to mark the retirement of Herbert Purves in 1973. Muriel is fourth from the left.

Author's private collection

Chapter Eight

AFFLUENCE AND FRAGMENTING PRIORITIES IN THE 1950s

The year 1949 marked a turning point in New Zealand politics. The conservative National Party brought in political and social changes. The principles of private enterprise and the free market superseded wartime controls in 1950. These changes brought Muriel's nutrition programme to a crossroads. The unity of purpose on nutritional issues that had existed under the Labour government since 1935 began to disintegrate. National had its own vision for the future of medical research, which was accompanied by a strong incursion of technology and science into everyday life and an emphasis on profit and economic prosperity. As a result, scientific research became 'purer' and more detached. Moreover, New Zealand medical and scientific research now had to compete on an international stage.

This period of growth and change, characterised by full employment, the development of a consumer society and improved communications, had significant consequences for the NZMRC and the NRD. The Medical Research Council Act of 1950 established the council as an autonomous research body. Like other NZMRC departments, it was expected to be self-sufficient and self-funding. Without the direct support of the Health Department, the NRD's public health schemes were no longer the highest priority in medical research.

The changes to the administration and funding of the NZMRC changed the direction of its research. In 1951 the NRD became the Nutrition Research Unit (NRU). Under Muriel's direction, the work of the unit focused on two main areas of investigation: the role of fats in causing coronary heart disease, and the role of fluoride in reducing dental caries.

In the newly prosperous 1950s, conditions related to dietary excess replaced the diseases of poverty and want as the focus of public health research (in the process shifting the emphasis from the health of working-class families to that of middle-class male executives). The sudden shift from under- to overconsumption was to some degree a measure of the success of the first generation of public health researchers in explaining and eradicating deficiency diseases.[1] At the same time, in the increasingly professionalised, competitive world of academic science and medicine, locally based public health research was being eclipsed by clinical medicine.[2] Policy-making became secondary to achieving academic respect. As a result, practical public health research became increasingly difficult to carry out within the new intellectual framework of medical research.[3]

A parallel social and political development was the valorisation of individual rights over community well-being. Not only was there resistance to participating in or funding collective health initiatives, but epidemiological research on class and social factors affecting health was dismissed in favour of an emphasis on individual responsibility and character.[4]

The 1950s promises of comfort, prosperity and stability came at a price, particularly for women. The ideal of the middle-class nuclear family placed women as permanent fixtures in the home with the primary responsibility for raising contented, emotionally well-nourished and socially well-adjusted children, while the husband and father served as the main breadwinner. This ideology of domesticity had long-term implications for professional women, especially in the sciences. The lack of opportunities and the sheer number of women graduates of the School of Home Science soon created strongly gendered fields of research.

Changes to medical research legislation also led to changes to the research programme of the NRU, although the continued presence of Muriel, Elizabeth Gregory and Charles Hercus meant that their public health concerns remained on the agenda. Muriel's old classmate Charles Burns replaced John Malcolm on the NRC in May 1949. Burns was a highly experienced physician who served as visiting physician and head of the cardiology department at Wellington Hospital from 1940 until

1966.[5] Muriel had recruited Burns for his expertise on the clinical aspects of nutrition, especially diabetes, alcoholism and the study of diet therapy. Dr F.B. Shorland, director of the Fats Research Laboratory, replaced Sir Theodore Rigg in January 1951. Rigg had served as a liaison with the Cawthron Institute, originally an independent technical institute for research into primary industries, and DSIR; Shorland's appointment signalled a new direction in research.

The NRU's areas of study in 1951 included a survey of foods eaten in New Zealand households, investigations into the vitamin and nutrient values of New Zealand foods, nutritional aspects of dental caries, vitamin C deficiency, nutritional problems of the Pacific Islands, anaemia and protein nutrition, nutritive values of Pacific Island foods, constituents of animal fats, and measurement of the vitamin content of fish-liver oils.[6] The unit took advantage of a visit by Sir Edward Mellanby, the former chair of the British Medical Research Council, to confer with him on research policy. Mellanby, who in 1917 had demonstrated that rickets was a deficiency disease, endorsed this programme and applauded the testing of fish-liver oils as a great public service.[7]

Pacific Islands research

Concerns about health in the southwest Pacific Islands, particularly Fiji and Samoa, were mounting in the late 1940s. The expansion of air transport increased the threat of rapid transmission of infectious diseases. The war in the Pacific had also increased interest in social and economic development in the region, for which New Zealand now had new administrative responsibilities.[8] In 1946 the New Zealand government initiated the Island Territories Research Committee to promote research into health problems. Epidemiological investigations had the highest priority. Diseases of particular concern were filariasis (roundworm infections), tuberculosis and skin infections. The director of medical services for the South Pacific area, Dr J.M. Cruikshank, had requested a nutritional survey in response to claims of a series of nutritional 'errors', especially macrocytic anaemia and dental caries in Fiji and protein deficiency in Samoa.[9] Funded by the British Colonial Development

Fund and the Island Territories Research Committee, an expedition was mounted to give an overview of the health, social and economic development challenges facing the island territories. The nutrition section of the expedition was responsible for investigating protein, mineral and vitamin deficiencies.

The survey was conducted over the long university summer holiday, and in January 1950 Muriel and Dr Lucy Wills travelled to Fiji and Western Samoa to study the local diets. Wills was a British haematologist who had worked in India, Jamaica and South Africa, and was well known for her research on folic acid, also known as the 'Wills factor'.[10] She had also investigated malnutrition in prisoner-of-war camps. Wills was a close friend of Margaret Hume, a nutrition researcher who worked at the Lister Institute with Harriette Chick. After retiring in 1947, Wills continued to work on nutritional problems and engage in local politics. Muriel most likely met her while working at the Elizabeth Garrett Anderson Hospital during the early 1930s, when Wills was superintendent there, and felt very fortunate to have her company on the expedition.

Although the initial plan was to survey all of New Zealand's Pacific Island territories, because of lack of space on the ship, the dietary survey was confined to Samoa and Fiji.[11] The topics of investigation included serum protein levels, haemoglobin levels, and the incidence of goitre and dental caries.[12] The researchers found that serum protein values were high among Fijians, Indians in Fiji and Samoans, in strong contrast to Europeans living in Fiji and Indians in India.[13] Lucy Wills urged, but without success, that the information obtained from the survey should be used to clarify whether high serum protein values (associated with skin diseases) indicated insufficient protein intake.

A nursing sister from New Zealand and a Fijian nurse accompanied them on their visits to Fijian villages, the latter acting as translator. They travelled around in a van that was fitted with cupboards, sterilisation equipment and basic medicines – a new idea in the Pacific – which allowed them to visit districts where the people were too poor to travel to hospital. To reach more remote villages, they went by horseback or boat. On their arrival, the local chiefs welcomed them with ceremonial kava drinking rituals and sometimes with gifts of bananas and coconuts.[14]

The racial and cultural differences between Fijians and Indians living in Fiji provided opportunities for research into infant feeding, especially in relation to protein levels, and pre-eclampsia (toxaemia of pregnancy).[15] Pre-eclampsia appeared to afflict only Indian women in Fiji: Samoans, Fijians, New Guineans and Solomon Islanders were not affected. Medical investigators acknowledged the many differences between the cultures: Fijians had a more communal lifestyle, whereas Indians living in Fiji were urbanised. In their paper, Muriel and Lucy Wills wrote: 'Their freedom from these disorders of pregnancy seems to indicate that something in their way of life is more right than something is in ours, and the circumstance is worthy of further study.'[16] Both believed that nutritional differences played a significant role. They observed that the Fijian diet included a large proportion of vegetables, which supplied the body with vitamins A, C, E and K in pregnancy, while the Indian diet was low in green, leafy vegetables and therefore lacked these vitamins. Muriel believed that further research in Fiji could reveal ways to prevent pre-eclampsia, but no additional time or resources were available.[17]

Consistent with her attempts to promote the consumption of milk in New Zealand and abroad, Muriel attempted to introduce the use of infant formula in the Pacific, using New Zealand skim milk. She noted that after weaning, infant mortality was higher among Fijian babies, who were fed bananas and coconut, than among Indian babies, who were fed milk. Although she encouraged the use of local foods for infant nutrition as far as possible, she argued that skim milk was the best food for infants because of its high protein level. 'It seems a pity that they have to try to make up formulae from fish and local foods when we have skim milk being discharged into rivers and the sea in New Zealand.'[18] The local availability and price of New Zealand powdered milk, however, were significant obstacles.[19] Soya beans were a possible substitute.

In a joint report on the nutrition of Fijians and Indians in Fiji, Muriel and Lucy Wills clearly stated that the reason for the high infant mortality rate in Fiji was not 'the biologically unlikely idea, so often repeated, that "Fijian mothers lack maternal instinct".'[20] They also expressed concern about the high cost of animal protein for Indian families and suggested a family planning campaign to reduce the number of high-risk pregnancies in the Indian community. The remainder of the Fiji trip focused on protein-deficiency anaemia, vitamin deficiencies and dental caries.

Muriel went on alone to study nutritional habits in Samoa while Lucy Wills remained in Fiji. Muriel enjoyed Samoan hospitality, which included a welcome ceremony when she arrived in the villages and a traditional Samoan meal, with singing and dancing the siva, after the examinations. Despite enduring hurricane conditions, she was able to carry out useful work. As in Fiji, mobile vans were the only way of providing medical services to people in the villages. Committees of Samoan women were responsible for caring for the sick in specially built houses and for organising people to seek treatment at the vans.[21]

Muriel listed the most severe health problems of the southwest Pacific Islands as kwashiorkor, anaemia, protein deficiency, pre-eclampsia, goitre, dental caries and the size and weight of children. In the last section of an article about her experience in the Pacific, published in *Nutrition Reviews* in 1956, she paused to ponder the wider benefits of such studies: 'Out of such studies may come important slants on the errors of our own way of living. Obviously, the Island people have something to teach us about immunity to disorders of pregnancy and to dental caries, even though we can help then with some of our information about infant feeding. Grateful as I am to our [laboratory] rat colony for the tales it tells, "the proper study of mankind is man."'[22]

The only follow-up work from the survey for the NRU, however, was to undertake some Pacific Island food analyses on request. The NRU did not have sufficient staff to carry out detailed analyses of foods, so the South Pacific Commission laboratory in Noumea took over the investigations. The Pacific Islands research work marked the end of a thirty-year era during which Muriel concerned herself with maternal and infant malnutrition.

Heading to Harvard

Muriel returned to Fiji at the request of the Medical Department two years later, on her way to spend part of her sabbatical year at Harvard University. Her sabbatical had been long deferred because of postwar stringency, and she was looking forward to investigating a number of nutritional subfields simultaneously at a world-class research institution. Muriel left New Zealand in late June 1952. Alf did not join her, preferring to backpack independently through Europe, and although they were in contact during their travels, they did not meet. Muriel headed via Fiji and India to Europe, where she attended the International Dietetic Congress in Amsterdam – the first of many meetings with nutritional scientists from all over the world.

In Britain Muriel visited a number of laboratories doing nutritional studies to learn about new equipment and techniques, 'particularly with reference to tropical foods, chromatography, studies on vitamin D, techniques of vitamin assay'.[23] In the Netherlands, Sweden, Denmark, and on both coasts of the United States, she visited laboratories involved with processing and distributing liquid milk. In this capacity she represented the Central Milk Council (soon to become the New Zealand Milk Board), which had provided her with a £200 travel subsidy. Muriel was impressed with the number of completely covered delivery vans, which made her feel 'somewhat ashamed of this particular aspect of the New Zealand Town Milk Industry'.[24] The council had also asked Muriel to enquire after the manufacture of yoghurt and whether it was possible to obtain a yoghurt culture.[25]

After spending the rest of the Northern Hemisphere summer in Britain, Muriel spent the remainder of the year in the United States. Her main objective was to sound out opinions on the recommended allowances of specific nutrients advocated by the Food and Nutrition Board of the US National Research Council: 'It is important that we should have some idea of the underlying currents of thought that have influenced the past decisions and of the changes that are taking place in the viewpoints held, for the Recommended Allowances have had a far-reaching influence on all phases of nutrition work throughout the world.'[26]

Beginning in September 1952, Muriel spent six months at the Harvard School of Public Health in Boston as a research fellow in nutrition. This position allowed her to undertake laboratory work and to attend lectures given by the head of the department, Frederick J. Stare. She recounted Dr Stare's 'thought-provoking' opening lecture, in which he pointed to the rapid changes in public health in the first half of the twentieth century:

'The student of public health must realise that the diseases of which people die today are not typhoid, pneumonia, scarlet fever, diphtheria or even tuberculosis, but atherosclerosis.'[27] With rapid advancements in treatments with antibiotic drugs and immunisation, degenerative diseases had supplanted infectious diseases as the primary concern in public health research. Stare's first series of lectures covered such topics as recent dietary surveys, nutritional education, the effect of climate on nutrition, and means of improving the world's food supply.[28]

Stare had founded the Nutrition Department at the Harvard School of Public Health in 1942 and served as its chair until 1976. He was the founding editor of *Nutrition Reviews* and wrote a column titled 'Food and your health'. He was well known in the scientific community and among the general public. He had represented the United States in the planning to prevent starvation in the Netherlands at the end of the war, once the German troops had retreated. After the war, when deficiency diseases had almost disappeared and medical interest in nutrition was waning, Stare refocused nutrition research at Harvard on the relationship between nutrition and atherosclerosis.

From September 1952 to February 1953, Muriel worked as first assistant in the laboratory of Dr D. Mark Hegsted. With Joseph J. Vitale, Hegsted was doing research on studies of enzymes, respiration, the relationship of caloric intake to protein and thiamine levels, and the effect of folic acid antagonists (antifolates), substances used in chemotherapy that interfere with the metabolism of folic acid, thus producing symptoms of folic acid deficiency. Hegsted assigned Muriel to study the metabolism of the amino acid glycine, using a radioactive marker. Through introductions made possible by her Otago Medical School research colleague Walter Edwin Griesbach, Muriel also visited other laboratories at the New England Medical Center and the Tufts University Medical and Dental schools, as well as the laboratory of Dr Dewitt Stetten Jr, chief of the Division of Nutrition and Physiology of the Public Health Research Institute of the City of New York. She was thereby able to compare the radioactive isotope work in progress at these institutions.[29] She also studied the use of an amino acid labelled with a radioactive carbon isotope as a means of investigation of 'protein turnover', a leading subject in the field at that time.[30]

Among the many differences between medical research in New Zealand and the United States, funding was the most obvious. Lack of funding prevented the NRU from taking on important survey work for the Food and Agriculture Organization. At Harvard, research into alcoholism, cancer, atherosclerosis and obesity were funded by large grants from private firms. 'At a Nutrition Conference on Obesity', reported Muriel, 'I heard that Insurance Companies and commercial food companies in USA were planning to spend five million dollars in combating obesity, which is a predisposing cause of diabetes, atherosclerosis, high blood pressure and cardiovascular-renal disease.'[31] Muriel was amused to learn of the existence of an organisation called Fatties Anonymous, and in general she noticed that much attention was devoted to weight loss.[32] The famous American obesity expert Dr Elliott P. Joslin described how he used to carry two pails of water in each hand to illustrate the burden of excess weight.[33] As a result of American work on the nutritional aspects of atherosclerosis, the Nutrition Research Committee recommended that New Zealand undertake work in this field.[34]

At Harvard Muriel was also able to pursue another question of importance to New Zealand: the causes of dental caries. Stare was an early vocal advocate of fluoridation of water supplies and frequently testified in support of it. These exchanges reinvigorated Muriel's interest in the problem. 'I feel that it is incumbent on our department to take up the subject once more', she concluded. 'The attitude that I have found here is that it needs much more data of all kinds before we shall be able to elucidate this complex problem.'[35]

Working at Harvard was stimulating, allowing Muriel to observe a variety of experimental methods among the sixty or so researchers in Stare's research group. It also enabled her to attend meetings and symposia in Boston. Muriel made herself useful in teaching biochemical and physiological theory, and delighted in the opportunity to lecture on her work in Fiji and Samoa and to describe the work of the NRU. Overseas researchers showed great interest in her work on improving bread, dietary surveys, Hercus's work on goitre, research on rosehip syrup and work to improve the welfare of children. Muriel ventured so far as to say, 'I think I can also claim to have tinctured it with a little of the ambassadorial element, which does not come amiss at the present juncture' (probably referring to the signing of the Anzus treaty in 1951).[36]

After her six months at Harvard, Muriel spent a month at the National Institutes of Health in Bethesda, Maryland. There she met Klaus Schwarz who was investigating liver function, specifically the role of 'factor 3', which he discovered to be selenium.[37] The New Zealand Soil Bureau was able to make use of Schwarz's discoveries in its investigations. Selenium was identified as another trace mineral largely absent in New Zealand soils, and selenium supplementation greatly increased the efficiency of New Zealand sheep farming, resulting in healthier stock, higher lambing rates and heavier fleeces. 'As in many other instances', Muriel later wrote, 'the animal stands as a buffer between soil deficiencies and human deficiency disease.'[38]

Muriel kept in regular contact with Schwarz following her visit, exchanging papers on selenium and later on the role of chromium in diabetes. Schwarz noted a side benefit of this correspondence: his sons all had impressive stamp collections, including specimens from New Zealand.[39]

Fats and cholesterol

The implication of animal fats in atherosclerosis and other degenerative diseases created a tension for New Zealand nutrition researchers between ensuring a healthy economy, on the back of a profitable export trade in butter and other animal fats, and a healthy population. The NRU's involvement in this field of research was driven by the growing influence of the research of American scientists on public opinion, such as the work of Ancel Keys on the role of fats and cholesterol in heart disease. Keys, a physiologist who specialised in nutrition, published work showing a correlation between high blood cholesterol levels, a diet high in saturated fat and coronary heart disease. His theory that reducing cholesterol could prevent heart disease earned him a place on the cover of *Time* magazine on 13 January 1961. Keys based his research on comparative investigations in Italy, where olive oil was used for cooking in the south and animal fats in the north. He hypothesised that a diet high in unsaturated fatty acids prevented the body from producing saturated fats, which combine with cholesterol to form arterial plaque and led to degenerative heart disease. It remained unclear whether the disease was caused by an excess of saturated fat or a lack of unsaturated fat, and what role the lowering of blood cholesterol played in preventing the disease.

Muriel considered that Keys' research neglected the changes in lifestyle that had occurred in the 1950s. She alluded to many of these in her talk, 'Maintaining the health of the middle-aged executive', at the British Medical Association conference, held in New Zealand for the first time in 1961. The influence of cars, reduced exercise and an increase in obesity all had detrimental effects on people's health. This line of reasoning challenged the contemporary belief in inexorable progress through technology and science. In challenging the new scientific consensus, she asked, 'How much is the car, not the cow, to blame?'[40] In her view, one of the key factors associated with the rise in deaths from atherosclerosis between 1927 and 1957 was the rise in prosperity. Both the World Health Organization and the Food and Agriculture Organization suspected that fat was a prime factor in causing this disease. Dubbed the 'industrial disease of the leader class', atherosclerosis made world news when the American president, Dwight D. Eisenhower, was diagnosed with it in 1956.[41]

In New Zealand, Muriel collaborated with F.B. Shorland on research on the metabolic aspects of fat consumption and accumulation. Shorland's discovery of the branched-chain fatty acids in butter and meat led to investigations of their nutritional value. Shorland had asked the Nutrition Research Unit to do the preparation and feeding of his laboratory rats, so that, according to Muriel, 'the incursion into the cholesterol problem was accidental on [NRU's] part'.[42] The collaborative research sought to investigate all the effects of animal fats on blood cholesterol levels, and specifically whether branched-chain fatty acids lowered cholesterol.[43]

Concerns about the adverse health effects of animal fats were of special importance to the dairy and meat industries of New Zealand. The Nutrition Research Committee noted, 'It is proper that these investigations on butter and fats, commodities which are of great economic importance to N.Z. should be done in our own country.'[44] According to Muriel, the economic dependence on trade in butter and meat, particularly with Britain, meant that 'we should make it number one priority to find out the yea or the nay of this sweeping statement [that animal fat is particularly to blame for arterial degeneration] ... New Zealand should stand on her own two feet when it comes to a matter in which her overseas trade is involved.'[45] If animal fats were shown to have a significant causative role in heart disease, New Zealand's economy would require a complete reorganisation.

Muriel's scepticism towards this theory fitted neatly with the interests of the butter industry. Its main competitors were US producers of corn oil and other plant oils. In December 1957 the *British Medical Journal* reported on the statement made on World Health Day that 'the time may come when we shall have to abolish the cow.'[46] This could be seen as an instance where, instead of taking a public health point of view, Muriel put economic consequences first. 'I shivered and shook', she commented, 'on behalf of our Dairy farmers, and of our Town Milk Producers, and the rest of us whose occupations, like mine, are dependent on the funds that flow from exports derived from sheep, cattle, cows, and grass – our life-blood as it were.'[47]

Muriel had been researching the beneficial and toxic roles of fats, particularly fish-liver oil, since her studies in the early 1930s at University College in London. Her advice remained essentially pragmatic. In her opinion the problem lay more with the accumulation of human fat than with the consumption of animal fat. There was a clear association between obesity and heart disease. 'The only glands involved in obesity', she said, 'are the salivary glands.'[48] While she agreed that too much fat in the diet was not good, the particularly harmful effects of animal fat were unproven; and until they were, she avoided a definitive judgement. 'We can't say yes it does, and we can't say no it doesn't.'[49]

Muriel highlighted 'how little we know about ourselves or about the question of dietary fat in relation to atherosclerosis'.[50] Her cautious approach to this question derived from her training under John Malcolm. She knew that the human body could make cholesterol much faster than it could absorb it from food. She was inclined to take a broader view of the issue, identifying the roles of all the constituents in fat. The usual approach of studying only blood cholesterol levels pointed, in her opinion, to a lack of understanding of the human metabolism: 'For my part, my mind is very full of questioning as to whether recent generalisations are justified as to the influence of unsaturated fatty acids – but it is merely because I think there are many more constituents of fat that we should explore. As a physiologist I am inclined to take the view that much has still to be explored.'[51]

Muriel's case was hampered not only by a shortage of research funds but by a lack of data on the actual intake of fat and calories in New Zealand and its relationship to the development of atherosclerosis. It was well known that New Zealanders consumed large quantities of butter and meat fat, but obesity statistics did not exist. In the late 1940s Muriel had approached insurance companies in an effort to obtain information on the proportion of overweight persons, but in 1957 she could still report no progress on this avenue of research. Charles Burns, Muriel's old classmate and a former member of the NRC, supported her: 'I am very interested in the question of intake of calories and of fat by the average person in the community, which obviously you would like to take up. This is a subject which is very much in the minds not only of the ordinary man who gets a coronary thrombosis, but in the minds of our legislators who are not free from this disorder.' He shared Muriel's desire to 'get to grips with this subject in a land which is so rich in animal fat, and which produces so much coronary atheroma.'[52]

Members of the NRC were beginning to feel frustrated by a lack of funding to pursue this initiative. Shorland observed that in the absence of adequate funding, the committee lacked authority and functioned in a purely advisory capacity.[53] Another colleague who sympathised with her situation was Dr Neil Begg, medical adviser to the Plunket Society. Begg approached Hilda Ross, the minister of social welfare, who in turn approached the minister of health on her behalf. 'Dr Bell is anxious to do research into butter to refute the American statement that some of our butter is poison. She is very despondent and greatly distressed at being unable to do the work which is so dear to her heart, and in which she is specialist and is most efficient.' It seemed the letter was passed to Harold Turbott, then deputy director general of health, who noted by hand: 'As far as I am concerned it is inaccurate.'[54]

In general Muriel received little public acclaim for her work, with the notable exception of her advice given to Sir Edmund Hillary and his New Zealand team of polar explorers and sled dogs on the Commonwealth Trans-Antarctic Expedition. This took place from 1955 to 1958, with the aim of making the first overland crossing of Antarctica via the South Pole. In this role Muriel was following in the footsteps of Malcolm, who nearly thirty years earlier had advised Admiral Richard Byrd on maintaining the health of his dogs en route to the South Pole. Byrd had been feeding them a type of pemmican (a combination of dried meat and fat) that was too low in calories and high in roughage, which caused diarrhoea in the dogs.[55] A Dunedin firm undertook to make a specially blended form of pemmican for Byrd's dogs, which made it possible for the expedition to proceed.[56] For the 1956 expedition, Muriel fished out Malcolm's recipe, which he had noted on the back of an old envelope, and completed the necessary analyses. The NRU supervised the manufacture of the food in Dunedin, and their advice was 'put to the practical test' on the polar plateau in 1956. The dogs succeeded in transporting Hillary to the pole and back in good shape, and Hillary claimed that his dogs 'looked splendid alongside the British ones'.[57]

The diet of the explorers was equally important, and Muriel was responsible for checking the menus for calorie content and nutritional value. A good supply of vitamin C was essential to the success of the expedition, as proved by Robert Scott's fatal expedition in 1910–11. The 1956 explorers secured an adequate supply of vitamin C from fresh fruit, vegetables and blackcurrant jam. In addition, the men took vitamin C tablets.[58] Embracing practical housewifely traditions, Muriel whipped up a batch of marmalade for them. She was proud to share in the success of her fellow New Zealanders and to point to the role that science had played in it: 'Not so long ago our analysis and our advice were put to the practical test in the Antarctic … And just as we can say with regard to the Antarctic … "New Zealanders can do it", so we can say New Zealand scientists, whether they do nutritional research or anything else, if you give them the opportunity, they can make discoveries in laboratories just as anybody else.'[59]

Years later at her retirement luncheon, some of the Antarctic explorers came up to her and said, 'When we open the Antarctic to women, you're going to be our first guest.' Muriel wagged her finger at them and said, 'I shall certainly keep you to that.'[60]

Chapter Nine

'BATTLE-AXE BELL': THE FIGHT FOR FLUORIDATION

At the end of Muriel Bell's term as director of the Nutrition Research Unit, in 1964, the NRC acknowledged that her 'most outstanding work in the field of research has been in relationship to dental caries'.[1] She was praised not only for her direction and supervision of research but also for the role she played in bringing about the public acceptance of fluoridation as a necessary measure to improve dental health. This achievement, however, required years of determined effort by Muriel and other public health officials.

Muriel had given herself the nickname 'Battle-Axe Bell' because of the years she spent 'battl[ing] for all sorts of food items in the course of trying to promote the health of women and children'.[2] She had meant it in jest, but there was an element of truth to it: 'She gave the impression at times that she enjoyed fighting and scheming.'[3] Muriel had waged battles in favour of more nutritious bread, safe milk and iodised salt, but none was as fierce as her campaign for water fluoridation. The issue exposed the gulf between the work of nutrition researchers and the public understanding of science. It was shaped by social, cultural and political as well as scientific change. The epitome of a well-documented debate about science in the society of the mid-twentieth century, the water fluoridation controversy also sheds light on the lived experience of a scientist in New Zealand society.

Once US researchers had established that fluoride could prevent dental decay, the battle began to implement fluoridation of public water supplies in New Zealand. This was the main research focus of the NRU from the 1940s to the 1960s, and the most ambitious public health measure of Muriel's career. Her belief in using science to contribute to the public good and her professional commitment to data-based public health policy placed her at the centre of a debate over the role of science in a progressive democracy.

The proposal to add fluoride to water supplies was a national policy that entered into private homes and bodies, and as such it met with a wall of opposition. The New Zealand public no longer widely accepted government intervention as 'the appropriate means of addressing all aspects of human need'.[4] A contemporary observer noted: 'The confidence which had existed in the state in the 1930s had disappeared to the degree that all forms of propaganda were viewed with suspicion. This had been the result of dictatorships in Nazi Germany and Communist Russia in the twentieth century.'[5]

Under Muriel's leadership, an early campaign for water fluoridation had begun in the mid-1940s. She devised a strategy that incorporated both laboratory research and community participation. The department would analyse the fluoride content of teeth and water in a locality and, at the same time, approach parents and town councillors for their support of water fluoridation.

Muriel's first efforts to collate evidence in support of fluoridation, undertaken with the assistance of Marion Harrison, were valuable in helping to build public support for the long-term use of fluoride. In a pilot scheme, she began distributing fluoride solutions to volunteer households to add to their water in 1944. The solutions were soon replaced with tablets, as they were easier to distribute. The participants included the future Nobel Prize winner John Eccles, then professor of physiology at Otago Medical School.[6] The number of families with young children using the fluoride tablets by the late 1950s generated some positive community opinion in favour of water fluoridation. Soon fluoridation of public water supplies was proposed as a public health measure.

Muriel introduced the public to the subject in three *Listener* articles published in August 1944. The first two articles discussed the role of excess fluoride in causing mottled teeth, while the third article considered fluoride as a means of protecting teeth from decay. She documented the shortage of fluoride in New Zealand water and New Zealanders' teeth and proposed a means of testing water fluoridation as a remedy. She suggested choosing two cities with the same water supply and bringing the fluoride level up to one part per million in one town in order to study changes to teeth.[7] The first proposal for trial fluoridation in 1945 in New Zealand, however, was unsuccessful.

In 1946 came a progressive move with the appointment of J.P. Walsh, an Australian, as dean of the Otago Dental School. He envisioned major changes to the school, encouraging postgraduate study and more collaborations with researchers in medicine. He was also charged with establishing a research programme, and when the NZMRC first set up the Dental Research Committee, it appointed Muriel as a member. She was able to guide Dr R.E.T. Hewat, field research officer to the Health Department's Division of Dental Hygiene, and later Mr T.G. Ludwig, together with colleagues in the Soil Bureau, into 'areas of enquiry which have since proved to be so rewarding'.[8] Muriel was thus instrumental in facilitating cooperation between the dental researchers, soil scientists and nutrition researchers of the early 1950s.

In March 1951 the US surgeon general stated, 'During the past year our studies have progressed to the point where we could announce an unqualified endorsement of the fluoridation of public water supplies as a mass procedure for reduced tooth decay by two-thirds.'[9] The following year a trial fluoridation scheme was proposed in Hastings to see if these results could be replicated in New Zealand. The town's mayor and councillors were enthusiastic about the scheme, which began in 1953.[10] The Hastings trial was a major step forward for the campaign, and Muriel congratulated the councillors for their progressive approach to public health.

During the trial, however, opposition began to emerge. It was based on two main arguments: first, that fluoridation was dangerous, and second, that even if it was not, it should not be compulsory. 'Freedom or compulsion?' read one anti-fluoridation advertisement.[11] The alleged ill effects of fluoridation ranged from skin inflammation, cancer and deafness to impaired memory in children, but there was no scientific evidence to support these claims.[12] Contemporary observers found that 'the pattern of opposition … was almost identical with overseas experience'. Anti-adulterationists, anti-compulsionists and naturopaths, who had similarly opposed vaccination, milk pasteurisation and water chlorination in the past, now turned their efforts to the supposed new dangers of fluoride in the water.[13] The medical officer of health for Palmerston North, Dr Derek Taylor, stated: 'From the earliest years of fluoridation there has been a small number of scientists, dentists and doctors with some misgivings on the subject. These men and women have been widely quoted, misquoted and part quoted by fluoridation opponents who have also used them to support their contention that "the experts disagree".'[14] In response to this opposition, the Health Department began a series of newspaper advertisements in support of fluoridation in newspapers. Broadcasts also featured on local radio in conjunction with the Dental Association.

The commission of inquiry

In 1956 the government appointed a commission of inquiry to investigate the issue of water fluoridation. The chair was Wilfred Stilwell, judge of the Arbitration Court; the other members were Percy Stainton, a merchant, and Norman Edson, professor of biochemistry at Otago Medical School. Edson had worked with Muriel since the 1930s, and they were well acquainted. His membership on the commission was no doubt advantageous to fluoridation advocates. Public hearings took place in Hastings, Auckland, Dunedin, Christchurch and Wellington.

The year leading up to the commission was a particularly difficult one for Muriel. During the 1950s Alf Hefford's health had deteriorated. Muriel dutifully cared for him, making him as comfortable as possible.[15] At times their relationship was strained, and they did not seem to display a great affection for one another.[16] Perhaps this was because Muriel and Alf, although both scientists, were very different people. Alf's conservative views must have collided with Muriel's mostly liberal ideas, especially those relating to gender roles and family life. In a series of letters Alf wrote to his daughter Cicely in the 1950s, he shared his experience of his marriage to Muriel: 'I'm inclined to think that marriages were not only more stable but, on the whole, happier in the bad old times when wives did not dream of questioning the accepted fact that they were the subordinate partner.'[17]

It was clear from the start of their marriage that Muriel put her work before her relationship and the conventional duties of a wife, but perhaps it was not until Alf came to Dunedin to live with Muriel that he felt the effect of these priorities. Although he did most of the household chores and gardening, Muriel sometimes liked to take things into her own hands, with varying degrees of success. Once she tried to disconnect the gas stove piping so that linoleum could be laid underneath it. She accidentally broke the pipe, forcing them to make do with Primus stoves – though she was still able to turn out a three-course meal.[18] On another occasion Muriel had done some heavy outdoor work, including road making, tree topping and patchwork cementing around the house during Alf's absence. In one letter, Alf wrote, 'Perhaps I've mentioned that she is much given to demonstrating that she's as good as a man – if not a darned sight better.' Alf went on, 'Fortunately she seems to thrive on the strenuous life but I think she enjoys demonstrating how self sufficient she is.'[19]

Muriel's daily routine contrasted greatly with the domesticity that was expected of a 1950s housewife. Her house was messy, and she often brought work home with her in the evenings and on weekends. She was frequently absent from home, travelling to Wellington via train and ferry in connection with her official duties. Alf's description of Muriel's domestic mannerisms offers a unique insight into her home life:

> Muriel is a marvel. She has no trace of what might be called the aura of wifeliness, but she does excel in all the material ministrations of a home-maker, pampering me unnecessarily and rarely letting up for a few minutes from the various jobs about the house, over-working every part of her except her tongue, and consistently putting in over-time at the Med. School. The drawback to it all is that she never has time to do things tidily and to leave things tidy. I don't think she ever possessed that habit.[20]

During Alf's final illness he commented that she was embarrassing him 'with the amount of "mothering" I get – all in her strange off-hand manner, with the minimum of words.'[21] The fact that Muriel said little was perhaps less an indication of natural taciturnity than of unhappiness. A childhood friend with whom Muriel became friends again later in life recalled: 'When her [first] husband died, she felt unable to live alone, and shortly afterwards she married a very different man of "a higher class". It turned out to be a most unhappy alliance and just when it was near to breaking point, he died. Muriel had learned from this, [and] went on with her professional life which was highly successful.'[22] After Alf's death in 1957, Muriel continued to live alone in her St Clair home.

While the fluoridation commission of inquiry was gearing up, an increasing number of parents asked to have their children included in the fluoride-tablet experiment, presumably as a result of the increased publicity and the Health Department's education campaign.[23] The logistical and educational work of the campaign – including correspondence, supplying tablets and explaining how to fluoridate country water supplies – was time-consuming.

In addition, Muriel and many members of the Nutrition Research Committee were heavily involved in collecting and preparing material for the hearings.[24] Muriel prepared written submissions for the Hastings, Dunedin and Wellington sessions. Although Sir Charles Hercus was more familiar with the case of iodine supplementation than of fluoride, he dealt with the public health aspects of water fluoridation and expressed the opinion that the measure was both rational and safe.[25] Professor Elizabeth Gregory, now dean of home science, explained the reasons against using food rather than water as a vehicle for fluoridation, while Rex Malthus, a senior chemist in the NRU, spoke as one of the few parents who had had the opportunity of reading all the literature.[26] Muriel appeared before the commission in Hastings and Dunedin as 'the chief witness supporting fluoridation on questions of physiology, biochemistry, and toxicology and their applications in medicine'.[27]

When Muriel made her presentation to the commission at Hastings on 29–30 November 1956, her evidence embraced current nutritional studies, medical investigations demonstrating that fluoridation was a worthwhile and safe procedure, and the good fortune of Hastings in being selected for the pilot fluoridation programme ahead of the rest of New Zealand.[28] In addressing the issue of toxicity, she showed that the effect depended on the dosage, as with any ingested substance. As examples, she described the effects of ingesting inadequate, adequate, optimal and excessive quantities of iodine, vitamin A and vitamin D. Fifteen years earlier, she recalled, the Health Department had been reluctant 'to put the necessary amount of iodine into iodised salt, because of the medical scare-mongering that forecast that there would be an increase in the number of cases of toxic goitre if the salt was iodised to a higher level'.[29]

Muriel continued with an explanation of her research into the relationship between fluoride and tooth decay, and especially of reports in 1938–40 that linked better teeth with the addition of one part per million of fluoride to the water supply. She presented analyses of samples showing that both New Zealand water and New Zealanders' teeth were low in fluoride. Addressing concerns about excessive accumulations of fluoride in the body (a common cause of mottled teeth), Muriel cited evidence from studies at Harvard and the National Institutes of Health in the United States, a Danish study among industrial workers and a British aluminium manufacturing study, showing that the proposed fluoride level was not harmful to health. She also explained the body's mechanisms for protecting itself from harmful substances, for example by diverting excess fluoride to the bones or excreting it in urine.

In a supplementary statement made at the Dunedin session of the commission, Muriel cited the words of Fred Stare: 'Certainly, fluoridation of public water supplies is one of the most intelligent and forward steps in public health of this generation.'[30] Muriel pointed out that New Zealand was lagging behind the rest of the world in its indifference to a remedy for dental decay that was so widely used.[31] In conclusion, she remarked: 'New Zealand has in the past been rather proud of being in the forefront of schemes for promoting the health of the child. By contrast, in the matter of sponsoring the fluoridation of water for prevention of dental decay, it seems to be sadly lagging behind the rest of the world. It has come to the point where it almost disregards the most prevalent and widespread of its diseases, dental decay.'[32]

The strength of Muriel's evidence lay in her thirty years' research on the problem. Three scientific authorities – Dr Edward Roche (a physician representing the Auckland Division of the British Medical Association), Charles Burns and Elizabeth Gregory – confirmed her evidence. Muriel belonged to 'the body of witnesses supporting fluoridation … who supplied the great weight of orthodox scientific and technical evidence'. Under cross-examination she said that 'under all known health conditions and at all ages there can be no harm to anyone in this country by consuming water fluoridated to 1 ppm'. The commission regarded her statement as 'a very definite expression of opinion by a witness exceptionally well qualified to give it'. Hercus declared his complete support for Muriel's statement of scientific facts.[33] Further endorsements of water fluoridation by the scientific establishment came from Dr J.B. Bibby, director of the Division of Dental Hygiene of the Health Department, and Dr G.N. Davies, head of the Department of Preventive, Public Health and Children's Dentistry at the University of Otago Dental School.

Women played prominent roles as witnesses on both sides of the fluoridation debate. They included four New Zealand general practitioners who spoke in opposition to it. Although each doctor cited different empirical sources, they all concurred that it was harmful to health. Dr Elizabeth Mudie pointed to the researches of the Danish scientist Kaj Roholm on fluoride toxicity in an industrial setting.[34] Greatly influenced by the Australian naturopath and nutritionist Mira Louise, Dr Maud Fere outlined the arguments in such publications as *Fluoridation the Poisoner*.[35] Coincidentally, Louise was in New Zealand at the time of the commission hearings and gave highly critical testimony against fluoridation. She argued that fluoride should be added to the human diet by organic means, through the consumption of foods naturally high in fluoride, rather than chemical methods. After hearing Louise talk in February 1954, Alf Hefford stated, 'I never heard so much hooey talked from a public platform in my life. She appears to be doing very well out of it. It strengthens my conviction that the proportion of ignorant and gullible people in the population is very large.'[36]

The most prominent opponents of water fluoridation in the United States also joined the anti-fluoridation campaign in New Zealand. Dr Eva Hill based her evidence on the researches of the American investigators Drs Leo Spira and George Walbott.[37] Muriel had discounted Spira's researches as early as 1943. She referred to him as an 'armchair specialist' and stated unequivocally that his statements rested on an insecure foundation.[38] Hill brought evidence before the commission describing a condition referred to as Spira-Walbott syndrome, thought to be responsible for a range of neurological disorders ranging from varicose veins to nail biting.

With her thorough knowledge of the scientific literature, Muriel was able to discredit much of the evidence. Her opponents were often opposed to fluoridation on principle rather than on the basis of scientific fact. The commission found that there was no evidence of harm from fluoridation at the level of one part per million and concluded that the practice was safe.[39] In July 1957 the commission of inquiry released its report recommending that the issue of water fluoridation should be decided by local authorities rather than at the national level by the Health Department. Ultimately, it would be the responsibility of each town to implement the measure. The next two years, from the release of the report until the local referenda, were characterised by a fierce battle between supporters and opponents of water fluoridation.

Science in society

Until this point in her career, Muriel had not needed to publicly defend her scientific opinions or her expertise: within the profession, her results spoke for her. Throughout the fluoridation campaign, however, laypeople responded to scientific analysis with arguments based in fear and doubt. Fluoridation advocates had to rely on their social status and public recognition to establish confidence in their expertise.

The commission acknowledged that the opponents of water fluoridation, 'whether or not they appeared to have support from orthodox scientific principles', had the right to challenge 'the harmlessness of a highly technical proposal … a right which in our view should be regarded as a matter of the greatest importance at a time when communities are becoming increasingly dependent on the integrity of scientists'.[40] Themes of democracy, progress, medicine, public health and its relationship to science dominated discussions in the news media. The increasing efficacy of modern drugs to combat disease had not eliminated public scepticism toward medical science.[41] Moreover, evidence of the power of modern science heightened concerns that it required public consultation and oversight. Thus a relatively simple and effective measure for preventing tooth decay came up against strong public opposition.

The Health Department's initial approach to water fluoridation had been to persuade local governments of the benefits of fluoridation in the hope that they would decide to introduce the measure by their own authority. A concurrent public health education campaign conducted through community groups and organisations was designed to inform the public of the advantages of fluoridation.[42] The Health Department and local authorities were cautious about bringing the debate into the public arena for fear of inciting opposition, as had happened in the United States and during the pilot programme in Hastings. In hindsight, the Health Department considered their caution to be a great mistake, as it had allowed the opposition to gain public attention first and thereby gain a greater following.[43]

A number of scientific organisations, including the New Zealand Medical and Dental associations and the Otago Medical and Dental schools lent their support to the fluoridation campaign. For example, as representative of the Auckland Division of the British Medical Association, Dr Edward Roche stated before Auckland's Fluoridation Committee in October 1959 that 'the medical profession do not regard fluoride added to water as medication, but as the addition of a required nutrient to prevent our children from having starved teeth'.[44]

Despite this large body of orthodox opinion in favour of water fluoridation, opponents to the scheme were more successful in gaining public support. Consequently, the commission's support for water fluoridation was refuted by public opinion. The Dunedin Anti-Fluoridation Society was formed in February 1957, and its 'energetic secretary', Miss R.S. Andrew, organised petitions and placed advertisements in newspapers. Anti-fluoridationists also issued pamphlets to householders and sent letters to newspapers.[45] They emphasised the freedom of the individual to reject compulsory medication and claimed that fluoridation could be 'poisonous'. Marion Robinson commented: 'It was interesting to look at the people who were anti-fluoridation, who were absolutely obsessed that they were going to be poisoned – it was real.'[46]

Fluoridation opponents proposed various other causes for dental decay, many of them relating to general nutrition deficiencies and a lack of wholesome natural foods in the modern diet. One key campaigner, D.M. Robinson of Auckland, held the view that malnutrition was the root cause and therefore the source of the remedy.[47] Through their connections with opponents in other parts of the world, especially the United States, they could also point to strong opposition to fluoridation among doctors and scientists.[48] One of these was Sir Stanton Hicks, a graduate of Otago Medical School and emeritus professor of human physiology and pharmacology, who, doubting the safety of long-term fluoridation, advocated that it be provided only in tablet form to children up to eleven years of age.[49] According to the fluoridation advocates, there was no evidence to prove fluoride caused any health problems. On the other hand, the lack of long-term population studies meant that there was no evidence to refute such claims, either. Opposition to water fluoridation came to represent a substantial challenge to scientific orthodoxy in New Zealand society.

In this controversy, Muriel probably faced additional resistance because of her gender. One contemporary medical student later reflected on the near impossibility of combining scientific research with social change given the extent of ingrained gender discrimination: 'I am sure none of us realised just what was involved when scientists like Dr Bell accepted the social challenges arising from their scientific studies … The young men in our class, including, I suspect, those whose mothers were doctors or scientists, had little conception of the problems which had confronted women such as Dr Bell in their determination to succeed in the male-oriented world of medicine and science.'[50]

To Muriel, however, the stronger the opposition, the greater the challenge. She teamed up with the Plunket advisor, Neil Begg, to approach Plunket mothers to support fluoridation, and the mind boggles at what Muriel could have meant in response to an appeal from Wanganui in 1958 in which she apparently suggested 'that they should also go underground'.[51]

Although supporters of fluoridation had initially wanted to avoid public debate, to minimise the impact of unfavourable public opinion on the local referenda results, by late 1959 they had launched their own educational campaign. 'Specialists from the dental and medical schools addressed over 20 organisations and groups, including kindergarten mothers' clubs, parent teacher associations, and professional bodies.'[52] Muriel and J.P. Walsh, the dean of the Dental School, spoke in support of fluoridation at public meetings.

To counter the influence of the Dunedin Anti-Fluoridation Society, supporters formed the Otago Children's Dental Health Association, which distributed leaflets outlining the successful results of fluoridation in Hastings and began its own campaign of advertisements, speakers and letter writing. One leaflet, *The Reason Why?*, contained the following message: 'Our growing bodies need many different foods in varying amounts, and must not be starved of any one of them. Every mother sees to it that her children's food, as well as being good and plentiful, is also well varied, to include all that is needed. But sometimes this aim is missed, for want of something in the local soil. So some areas have goitre, and some have bad teeth.'[53]

The fluoridation campaigners were able to point to the impressive results in Hastings after only three years of fluoridation. Investigators reported a substantial reduction in the prevalence of dental caries in children aged six to eight. These results were consistent with those from overseas. Thomas Ludwig, dental research officer for the Medical Research Council, reported that 'the amount of caries experienced by seven-year-old children in Hastings has been reduced by approximately thirty-nine percent and the amount experienced by eight-year-old children by approximately eighteen percent'.[54]

Local newspapers also influenced public opinion. Dunedin's two daily newspapers took opposing stances on fluoridation, the *Evening Star* in favour and the *Otago Daily Times* against. In 1957–58 there were 172 letters to the papers' editors in opposition and 102 in support.[55] From July 1957 to November 1959 the *Evening Star* printed 180 column inches of editorials on water fluoridation, while the *Otago Daily Times* printed 170. Both sides were preparing public opinion for the referenda on 21 November 1959.

In the event, in all eight towns that held referenda, water fluoridation was defeated. 'The results of the fluoridation polls throughout the Dominion will have come as a disappointment to those who have been advocating materialisation of a progressive health measure,' observed the *Evening Star*.[56] The editorial in the *Otago Daily Times* commented: 'In its zealous advocacy the Health Department particularly and other esteemed professional interests, overstepped the boundary which divides expert counsel from coercion.'[57] Muriel's hopes, expressed as early as May 1958, of a victorious celebration in the form of a 'wonderful bonfire of all the paper on fluoridation' had turned to ashes – at least for the time being.[58] According to one colleague, after the Dunedin campaign was finally won in 1967, Muriel ceremonially burned a stack of *Otago Daily Times* newspapers in her backyard.[59]

The 1959 referenda results showed that the public's views were at odds with those of the scientific establishment. Despite their advocacy for the public good, Muriel and her co-workers belonged to a scientific elite that operated at a distance from the general public. The Board of Health discussed the results at its meeting shortly afterward. Muriel 'took heart in the strength of the vote for fluoridation [8000 in favour] notwithstanding sustained newspaper opposition'. Board member Francis Maclean said fluoridation must go forward in the public health programme, the task being to educate members of local authorities and persuade them not to hold polls or be influenced by scare tactics. The committee chair recommended against condemning ordinary citizens who voted against fluoridation, since the average person did not have the time, inclination or ability to look fully into the matter. Part of the problem was that local authorities 'did not have sufficient faith in the principle of fluoridation' and left the decision to ordinary citizens. 'In some cases the proposal for a referendum had appeared almost as an invitation to reject fluoridation.'[60]

Water fluoridation represented an initiative by a progressive modern society to apply the latest scientific knowledge. But the experimental evidence that had been so successful in persuading the commission of inquiry had failed to convince the public. In fact, the more technical the language of the measure, the greater the local political opposition. As the political scientist Austin Mitchell commented, 'Defeat followed almost inevitably when the issue was put to a public vote, partly because it was difficult to persuade people of the necessity of a measure, the benefits of which were not immediate and obvious, and partly because it was easier for opponents of fluoridation to place doubts in the public mind than it was for supporters to remove them.'[61]

Muriel's stance on water fluoridation illustrates how she situated herself as a professional scientist and public health researcher. Providing understandable information to the public was a significant part of her work. Where a vitamin or mineral deficiency was causing a widespread public health problem, however, she staunchly advocated reliance on scientific expertise. By aligning herself with mainstream science, she asserted the credibility of the work of her research unit and effectively marginalised the anti-fluoridationists as 'diet cranks' and 'food faddists'. In her view, general practitioners opposed to water fluoridation represented the 'soft' science of naturopathy. Eva Hill had isolated herself from the medical community by publicly opposing water fluoridation, against the instructions of the British Medical Association.

Fluoridation advocates were optimistic that time would show the safety and benefits of the practice. As one newspaper article pointed out, 'New Zealanders as a whole have yet to feel the confidence which they are certain to gain in the years to come from the practical experiments undertaken in Hastings and in several other places where local administration has shown courage and vision.'[62] On a more philosophical note, another article commented: 'Resistance to innovations forms an interesting study in human short-sightedness, but it is more serious than that, for it has prevented medical services from keeping pace with medical knowledge.'[63]

In the early 1960s Muriel felt that much patience was still necessary, 'as will be revealed by our failures, as the tale of both success and failure unfolds'.[64] As Muriel was considering her options toward the end of her career in the Nutrition Research Unit, Burns advised her against declining an invitation to work in the United States solely on account of 'the fluoridation business'. 'Fluoridation has got going,' reasoned Burns, 'and it will gradually be accepted on a national scale. Time is the answer, not political log rolling, which gets us nowhere; after all truth and justice inevitably triumph, in spite of politicians and cranks.'[65]

Throughout the 1960s Muriel continued to collate the mounting evidence and court rulings in support of water fluoridation. The Health Department had learnt its lesson and worked assiduously to educate the public on the benefits of fluoride. A letter to mothers from the director general of health, Harold Turbott, had recommended fluoridation as a 'convenient, effective and a safe way of substantially reducing dental decay'.[66] Reaping the benefits of her early research involving fluoride tablets,

Muriel noted the simultaneous beginnings of 'good dental development' and 'favourable opinion … Also, reports from mothers are coming in, all in a favourable key. We hope that this will silently achieve our objective of fluoridation in the end.'[67]

Implementation of fluoridation schemes, however, was slow. By 1962 Muriel reported that only one town, Lower Hutt, had installed equipment for fluoridation.[68] She added regretfully, 'One could say much about the years that the locust has eaten; today's adolescents could have had good teeth if minds had been receptive in the mid-forties. Several other towns have decided in favor of fluoridation and are now awaiting the arrival of their equipment.'[69] In an article in the *New Zealand Medical Journal* in 1964, she stated: 'No one now disputes the advantages to the developing teeth of having fluoride at a concentration of one part per million in the water supply.'[70] In the same article, however, she asserted that 'it is the physiological and medical aspects of fluoridation on which issue is taken by opponents of this public health measure'.[71] She therefore continued her campaign to show that fluoridation improved dental health and caused no harm.

Ten years after the commission of inquiry, most New Zealand communities had fluoridated water.[72] Muriel's satisfaction was such that she compiled a map indicating the areas with fluoridated water to send out with her Christmas cards in 1965.[73] In recognition of her efforts toward water fluoridation, the New Zealand Dental Association made her an honorary member. It was the first time that honour had been extended to someone outside the dental profession.[74]

Chapter Ten

THE FINAL STRUGGLE

Muriel's work continued to gain recognition and influence. In 1952 she became a fellow of the Royal Society of New Zealand, and in 1959 she became a fellow of the Royal Australasian College of Physicians, the only New Zealander admitted that year. In recognition of Muriel's exceptional services to the profession, they waived the customary examination.[1] In addition, she was appointed Commander of the Order of the British Empire in 1959 in recognition of her lifetime of service to the field of public nutrition and public education on health. 'All her energies have been devoted to improving the national economy and promoting better health for our people ... In the field of nutrition, no one can match or even approach her contribution to the national welfare.'[2] The Otago University Association of Home Science Alumnae prepared a list of her outstanding contributions to the field of nutrition, including her work on bush-sickness in sheep, goitre, the milk industry and fluoridation. Her talent for health education was described as 'a unique ability to translate her high scientific knowledge into terms readily understood and appreciated by the layman', as shown in more than one hundred *Listener* articles on a vast array of nutritional topics during World War II.[3] New Zealanders had Muriel to thank for the introduction or improvement of wholemeal bread, whole-grain cereals, school milk and fish-liver oils. The World Health Organization recommended her book *Normal Nutrition*, a textbook for nurses first published in 1948. An extension of her lecture notes for senior nurses, the text was designed to promote further study in dietetics and stimulate interest in nutrition among nurses. As Charles Burns observed, 'It could scarcely receive any higher praise. This little book is a mine of information of the greatest value not only to nurses, but also to medical and dental students, as indeed to practising doctors; every aspect of nutrition is covered within its closely printed pages.'[4]

The end of school milk

In the 1960s policy approaches to public health and clinical medicine were shifting. This was partly because measures born of the Depression were no longer in keeping with the political and social programmes of governments and partly because of a culture that placed increased emphasis on individual freedom and responsibility. The World Health Organization's definition of public health was 'a state of complete physical, mental and social well-being'. In this spirit, the role of medical professionals had changed from autocratically treating patients to teaching individuals to take responsibility for their own health.[5] Reaching the individual as well as appealing to a sense of community became a double challenge for public health professionals. A generation of public servants who had grown up with the benefits of government interventions in public health, such as iodised salt and school milk, now saw these measures as encroaching on the freedoms of the individual. Community educational campaigns fell largely on deaf ears.

The growing opposition to the school milk scheme was a sign that large-scale preventive public health measures were no longer deemed necessary or appropriate. By 1960 many school board officials, parents and teachers considered that the original reasons for introducing the school milk scheme were no longer valid. They argued that parents were now able and willing to take full responsibility for their children's diet.[6] The Otago Education Board argued that today's 'affluent society' made efforts to ensure a more nutritious diet for children redundant.[7] Moreover, the milk scheme incurred costs for school boards, such as provisions for hygiene and refrigeration. Even some of those who supported school milk argued that it was needed only for children of primary-school age.

In addition, starting in the mid-1950s, opponents had begun to question the health benefits of school milk. Three Napier doctors suggested in the *New Zealand Medical Journal* that the Health Department's 'Drink more milk' campaign might be responsible for the rising incidence of allergies and respiratory problems among children. They also suggested that the high incidence of dental caries was correlated with the high consumption of dairy products. Criticising government subsidies on dairy products, they claimed: 'The matter is tied up with large commercial interests which are intent on forcing milk and milk products on the public. We think they would be better employed in selling the idea and their wares to the under-nourished Asiatics.'[8]

To the argument that school milk was not an effective way of improving child nutrition, Muriel responded with data showing an increase in the growth rates of children and adolescents in New Zealand and attributing the change to the increased consumption of milk.[9] She therefore favoured the scheme 'on the grounds of protecting the child's proper nutrition'.[10] Although she acknowledged that serious malnutrition in the absence of the scheme was unlikely, she did highlight increased physical stature as an overall improvement to the 'biological merit' of the nation.[11]

As to the argument that only young children needed milk, Muriel asserted that rapidly growing teenagers required more protein, calcium and vitamins than younger children. She further observed that milk was preferable to fizzy drinks and candy bars. It was curious, she observed, 'that in a country such as ours, which obtains part of its wealth by overseas sale of dairy products including cheese and dried milk – both derived from milk – that there should be some lack of awareness of the good food value there is in milk itself'.[12] Similarly, the argument that the current generation of children was better nourished was countered by experts who asserted that instant breakfast foods such as cornflakes were less nutritious than old-fashioned porridge.[13]

A new argument in favour of the consumption of milk was the role of calcium in preventing bone diseases such as osteoporosis. A researcher from Cornell University, Dr Leo Lutwak, expressed interest in coming to New Zealand to undertake a comparative study of the lifestyle of residents of the United States with that of New Zealanders. He aimed to investigate the effects on the aetiology of osteoporosis of habits like sedentarism, television viewing and spending time indoors. Alongside his theory that genetic predisposition could affect the body's capacity to absorb calcium in milk, he hypothesised that chronic lack of exercise has the effect of thinning the bones, and insufficient exposure to sunlight results in vitamin D deficiency, further weakening bone structure.[14]

Despite Muriel's efforts, the decision of the Hawke's Bay Education Board to end the school milk scheme in 1960 was the first of several similar moves by local school authorities.[15] In more impoverished areas such as South Auckland, however, 86 out of 160 school committees voted in favour of retaining milk schemes in some form.[16] Muriel was left to put her faith in the mothers of the nation: 'Though I have just witnessed the phoenix of school milk burnt in the fire, I feel that something will arise from its ashes. Mothers will see to that, I'm sure.'[17]

While some experts were questioning the health benefits of milk for children, others were drawing attention to the negative effects of animal fat on cardiac health for adults as well. *Time* magazine's 1961 cover article on coronary heart disease advised people to reduce their saturated fat intake as a preventative measure. Muriel took a great interest in the subject from the point of view of the dairy industry. 'We are not unmindful that the dairy industry accounts for a quarter of our national income. Added to this is the export of about [£]3 million sterling worth of tallow, plus all the fat in the meat we export.'[18] New Zealand's export trade during the early 1960s took on a special significance in light of the fact that Britain was negotiating with the European Economic Community.

Winding down at the NRU

As she approached retirement in the late 1950s, Muriel went on various trips abroad. She travelled partly to represent New Zealand at international meetings and partly to search for a successor. Her trip in 1960 was prompted by an invitation from the New Zealand branch of the British Medical Association to speak on the topic of heart disease from a nutritional point of view. Muriel hoped to use the opportunity 'to find out what viewpoints were developing which might be of moment not only therapeutically but also in the matter of our export market'.[19] Her application for travel funding was initially rejected because she had only two years of public service remaining before her retirement. The minister of health, H.G.R. Mason, intervened on her behalf, noting that Muriel would 'undoubtedly continue in public life for some years' and that 'Dr Bell is so deeply involved in nutritional matters in New Zealand that she feels she has a personal responsibility to make this overseas visit and proposes to do so even if Government assistance is not given'.[20] The decision was reversed and her application was funded.

Muriel was abroad from September to December 1960, during which time she attended the fifth International Conference on Nutrition in Washington, DC. In Aberdeen she visited the Rowett Research Institute and the Height and Stetric Research Unit of the Aberdeen Royal Infirmary, and discussed fisheries research with Dr Lovern, a contact of Jack Drummond's at the Torry Research Station. She visited the Ministry of Agriculture's Fisheries and Food Research Factory, where she saw 'their wonderful success with the meat bar and all sorts of other light-weight dried foods of such interest to Antarctic explorers and mountaineers'.[21] A German woman she encountered at a session on lipids introduced her to the idea that New Zealand's high-quality linseed oil could become a valuable export. She observed considerably more concern about dietary fats and cholesterol in the United States than in the United Kingdom, where the prevalent view was that there was no conclusive proof that animal fats caused coronary artery disease.

Muriel reported her findings on nutritional factors implicated in heart disease at the first New Zealand BMA conference, held in Auckland in February 1961, in an address alliteratively titled 'Calories, corpulence, cholesterol, coronaries, cows, corn, cars et cetera'. She reported: 'I should say at the outset that my pilgrimage did not result in finding clear answers to questions implied in the title.'[22] She emphasised that the relationship between cholesterol and coronary artery disease was not a simple case of cause and effect. She herself remained convinced that being overweight and inactive were the main factors contributing to heart disease, and that genetics might also play a role.[23] Consequently, she regarded reducing the intake of fats as an effective means of losing weight but not as a means of preventing heart disease.

Muriel gave short shrift to dietary theories from the United States and placed greater emphasis on research such as a British study on the different rates of heart disease in bus drivers and bus conductors. The latter had a lower incidence of thrombosis, which was attributed to their being more active during the working day. Research in the United States focused on experiments with laboratory animals to find out whether lowering calories from fats reduced blood cholesterol levels. Muriel was inclined to question this kind of research and to present its results as ambiguous. The NRU's studies in collaboration with Fats Research Laboratory had found that 'while corn depressed the level of blood cholesterol, some extra cholesterol seems to be present in the aorta as a consequence'.[24]

Another motivation for her travel abroad was to find a successor who would carry on her legacy as director of the NRU. In spite of worldwide recruitment and advertising, promising applicants for New Zealand positions were difficult to find. Furthermore, two Nutrition Research Committee members, Malcolm and Richardson, still had not been replaced. The field of nutrition was failing to attract brilliant young researchers. The agenda had changed: research scientists were no longer investigating the cause of rickets and other childhood deficiency diseases. Poverty, want and malnutrition had given way to plenty, excess and obesity. To make matters more difficult, the NRC insisted that the incumbent should have several years' training.[25] Muriel, moreover, insisted that she must train her successor personally.

Another impediment to recruitment was the fact that New Zealand research facilities and funding were not competitive with those in North America and Europe. Muriel's personal encounters with potential candidates may have done little to mitigate such concerns. An assistant of Muriel's recalled her turning up at laboratories in Cambridge in the early 1960s wearing an old sack dress and carrying a kete. She was apparently unaware that her appearance made New Zealand seem remote not just scientifically but also socially and culturally.

This was not the only occasion when someone commented on her fashion style, or lack of it. By this time her personal appearance was a long way from the sophisticated image she had projected in London in 1933. An old friend gave the following account of an encounter with Muriel:

> Her frugality was phenomenal, and I well remember being taken with her one evening to visit a colleague of hers in their charming home in Napier.

> Muriel sat there, happy and relaxed, dressed for a visit. She was wearing a dress she had made for herself, hem uneven and frock unattractive. She was wearing a pair of her late husband's socks and a pair of many-times washed and almost worn-out tennis shoes. An incredible appearance, but what struck me and this is why I am recording it, was the deep respect and might I say love that her hostess and host clearly showed they had for her. She was in every way a remarkable woman.[26]

Muriel's idiosyncratic dress sense can be seen as simply another example of her lack of interest in meeting others' fashion expectations, but it was also in part a matter of physical comfort. She often wore open sandals, for example, because of her hammer toes. Her disregard for makeup and fashion likely stemmed from her self-image as a highly acclaimed research scientist and medical doctor.

The closure of the NRU

In the event, Muriel's search for a successor was unnecessary. On 18 April 1963 the dean of Otago Medical School phoned Charles Burns to warn him of the very real possibility that the Nutrition Research Unit would not receive funding in the coming year. He noted that 'it was quite a fight to get the Research Council to agree a year ago to supporting your Department for this one year'.[27] Burns did not divulge the names of the people who favoured abolishing the department, which were given to him in confidence, but among those with competing interests for research funding was Muriel's old classmate Douglas Robb, now chancellor of the University of Auckland. Robb was no doubt interested in securing funding to establish medical research at the future Auckland Medical School. The British Medical Association's representative, Dr John Keeling, supported the NRU's continued existence and was instrumental in winning support for funding it for another year.

To resolve the issue, the NZMRC asked Sir Harold Himsworth, secretary of the Medical Research Council in Britain, to make a recommendation on the fate of the NRU, having dealt with an identical issue in the United Kingdom. At a special meeting of the NRC, Himsworth criticised Muriel's agenda for not 'working round a central core' as it had done with deficiency disease research during the days of the British nutrition researchers Frederick Gowland Hopkins and Edward Mellanby. He felt that Muriel and her staff 'were responding to demands rather than following a philosophy'.[28] Muriel responded by noting the many different fields of medicine with which nutrition research intersected and the need to have a research director who was capable of integrating these diverse fields of knowledge.[29]

Muriel's priorities in nutrition research had long been mothers and their need for accurate, sensible advice. The NRU was the authoritative source of all information that filtered down to mothers through hospital nurses, Plunket nurses and public health nurses. To abolish nutrition research, she felt, was to cut off the source of mothers' knowledge. As proof of the importance of nutrition research, Muriel cited the discovery in Karitane hospitals in 1938 that artificially fed babies in hospitals were developing scurvy because of vitamin C deficiency. She argued that research on problems that afflicted New Zealanders must take place in New Zealand, rather than reduce New Zealanders to acting 'like parasites, leaning on researches done in other countries'.[30] The lack of research on diabetes in New Zealand was a case in point.

The arguments for closing down the NRU cited the decreasing relevance of nutrition in modern medical science. It was true that nutritional science no longer held the status that it had in the 1930s, but as chairman of the Nutrition Research Committee, Muriel argued that it was 'inconceivable that the Medical Research Council should abandon a department that was considered a first essential when it was formed'.[31] She listed contemporary questions in nutrition and food safety to which there were no clear answers, like the therapeutic effects of radioactivity in foods (radioactive protein therapy), accelerated freeze drying (AFD) as a new method of food preservation in the meat industry, and the possible carcinogenic hazards of new synthetic food and beverage additives. Nutrition research had hardly lost its relevance. The research unit needed Muriel to continue in her function as 'a digester of information and a director of research'.[32]

Without a figure like Muriel at its head, the outlook for the unit was bleak. In a letter to Muriel, Charles Burns described her situation thus: 'One of your difficulties lies in that so to speak you are out on a limb, retaining a somewhat precarious existence only through your own personal eminence in this field … Never again will there be one so utterly dedicated to that subject which you have made your life's work; and anyone who chose to work in comparative isolation, in the way that you have been forced to do for various reasons, would just get nowhere.'[33]

Burns had defended the unit's importance at an NRC meeting in 1962, arguing that nutrition research was of prime importance to community health and the training of medical undergraduates, but that it had not been well integrated into the medical curriculum and that 'the broader issues of nutrition were lacking … It was difficult to change ways of life and more so if the medical profession as a whole was not geared towards a change.'[34] With heart disease becoming a high priority in medicine, the lipids research being undertaken by the NRU was of considerable importance. In late 1962 Burns urged Muriel to collaborate with the dean and the professor of medicine to prevent the unit from being closed down, 'for to whom should Nutrition be of surpassing interest if not the physician?'[35] Six months later, however, the unit's future was uncertain. The dean proposed that nutrition research be taken over by the Department of Physiology, which Burns believed was now 'the better choice, provided that there is a close linkage with Medicine and with Pathology and with Home Science.'[36]

Muriel's own time at the NRU was limited, as she would reach the mandatory retirement age of 65 in January 1963. She already had alternative career options: she had been invited to work as a guest in the Nutrition and Endocrinology Department at the US National Institutes of Health, an offer that she hoped would lead to a United States Public Health Service grant for a project on Pacific Island foods and the relationship between dental caries and soil nutrients. Tempting though this invitation may have been, Muriel's loyalty remained with her unit, and its survival became a cause in its own right.

Muriel spent May to September 1963 on another overseas tour, visiting a number of nutrition researchers and representing New Zealand at the World Food Congress in Washington, DC. The National Council of Women had recommended her to Prime Minister Keith Holyoake as a representative who was 'highly qualified in the field of nutrition, able to make a contribution to the Congress's consideration of one of the basic scientific and social problems which must be overcome if the people of the world are to live in peace and prosperity'.[37] While in the United States Muriel visited researchers working on fluoride, nutrition education and osteoporosis. She returned to Harvard and the National Institutes of Health in Bethesda before traveling to Britain, where she attended a conference of the Nutrition Society focusing on the interaction of trace minerals and nutrients. She also attended the Sixth International Congress on Nutrition in Edinburgh. Among the New Zealanders present were Elizabeth Gregory, Charles Burns, Charles Hercus, Elizabeth Neige Todhunter, Alice M. Copping and four dieticians.

It was while this conference was in progress, with several members of the NRU in attendance, that Himsworth gave his final recommendation to the NZMRC about the future of the unit. He acknowledged finding 'research of real quality in progress', but said that he had not been prepared for 'the high quality of research in progress in a considerable proportion of the places outside the Otago Medical School'.[38] Himsworth suggested a new structure for medical research, representing six essential scientific subjects: internal medicine, surgery, pathology, microbiology, physiology and biochemistry. In the words of F.B. Shorland, who delivered the first Muriel Bell Memorial Lecture, 'He told us that the classical era of nutrition had drawn to a close – all that was left belonged to biochemistry.'[39] According to Himsworth, the work of the NRU could be done in biochemistry or other departments. On the recommendation of Harold Turbott, the director general of health (in his capacity as MZMRC chairman), the NZMRC decided to disband the unit.

Marion Robinson, who had taken Elizabeth Gregory's place on the NRC after Gregory's retirement in 1962, recalled the situation with some emotion: 'Nutrition research died … You get that with Muriel Bell. When she retired the department went. It was terrible, Turbott killed it.' She noted, 'But what was saddest, this was done when [Muriel] was overseas at a meeting in Edinburgh. She was not there. It was very tragic, the whole thing.'[40]

Turbott had led a highly successful career as a public health administrator. Recognised internationally for his work on tuberculosis among Māori, he had served as a medical officer in New Zealand and the Pacific before entering the administrative hierarchy and becoming director general of health in 1959.[41] Despite the long-standing collegial relationship between Turbott and Muriel, Turbott's leading role in closing the NRU suggests some degree of personal rivalry or animosity. At the very least, his announcement of the NZMRC's decision at the Dieticians Association Conference in Christchurch, before informing Muriel personally, certainly attests to his insensitivity. The *Otago Daily Times* editorial referred to the 'lack of finesse which has become too often associated with the working of the Health Department's bureaucratic machine' and took issue with the closure. 'In the future the work of the present staff of the Nutrition Research Committee will be on projects backed on their merits by the MRC, rather than on long-term continued work.' This state of affairs seemingly left the researchers who had not been transferred to other MRC units 'free to engage in pure medical research'. Isolated nutrition projects were funded only for a further three years, 1965–68. Effectively the NZMRC's decision resulted in the abandonment of the nutrition research programme at Otago Medical School.[42]

In Edinburgh, Muriel took the opportunity to seek out the support and opinions of her international colleagues. She asked 'whether nutrition research had now disintegrated, and was met by shocked surprise at the query'.[43] New Zealand appeared not to be following international trends. In other parts of the world, nutritional science was gaining importance both as an independent science and within medicine. A British MRC grant had recently been given to the former Dunn Biochemistry Institute, the Dunn Nutritional Laboratory, at Cambridge.

Charles Burns recounted his last personal encounter with Muriel, shortly after the announcement of the disbanding of the NRU:

> She was a broken woman, and no words of mine were of any help, nor I would believe of consolation – because there was in fact nothing that at that point in time we could do about the situation. From that time onwards it seemed impossible to get close to her and even the decision to establish a Nutrition Research Society for New Zealand, which we thought would be received by her with joy, brought little or no response: her sense of justice had been so disturbed that it appeared as though she just wanted to be left alone with her thoughts, and her day to day tidying up of her Department.[44]

Letters of protest about the manner of the announcement came from NRC members Marion Robinson, Edward Sayers, James Robinson and Charles Burns, from Home Science alumnae and from the Plunket Society. Plunket's medical advisor, Neil Begg, stated that Muriel 'was a sheer anchor of common sense in all matters of nutrition'.[45] Affiliated organisations sent additional letters of support. The National Council of Women had been a supporter of nutrition research since the NRD's inception.[46] The Consumer Council, of which Muriel had been a member since its formation in 1959, sent a letter of support.[47] The professor of the School of Home Science, Patricia Coleman, presented a number of parliamentary questions for Ethel McMillan, MP for Dunedin North, to ask concerning the lack of other sources of advice on nutritional problems to such groups as the Adult Education Department and the Pan-Pacific Association, as well as answers to specific enquiries from doctors, nurses and the general public. 'What provision is being made for the continuation of research into human nutrition in New Zealand? Will Dr Bell's work in protection against food additives be adequately continued?'[48]

The Nutrition Research Committee condemned the decision to disband the NRU as a 'retrograde step'.[49] The unit, according to the committee, provided a combination of 'applied basic knowledge of medicine and chemistry coupled with active reading and research on nutritional problems together with an appreciation of the implications to the food and agricultural industries'.[50] Muriel had once cynically commented that politicians liked economic arguments, and her work withstood the test of political argumentation. Her research into bread manufacturing had shown how to provide the highest possible nutritive value at the lowest cost. The collaborative work with the Fats Research Laboratory in exploring the metabolic aspects of fat consumption and accumulation benefited the dairy and meat industries, which accounted for a substantial proportion of the New Zealand economy. In Muriel's mind, this work toward the understanding of fats alone justified the existence of a nutrition research unit in New Zealand. The 1930s adage 'The nation's health is the nation's wealth' reflected the importance of good public health to the national economy.

The closure of the NRU had close parallels with the shifting attitude towards home economics in the United States in the 1950s and 1960s. Leaders in home economics 'not only had to fight losing battles for personnel and resources but also constantly had to define and defend the field's intellectual rigor and social importance'.[51] The almost total feminisation of the field of nutrition made it vulnerable to departmental restructuring and weakened its standing in the sciences. The links between the NRU and the School of Home Science at Otago did little to strengthen the standing of the unit. This was a complete and ironic reversal of the situation at the beginning of Muriel's career, when the field of nutrition provided some of the first opportunities for women to become professional research scientists.

Nutrition research was by no means obsolete: as Shorland later noted, 'At the time of Dr Bell's retirement, Sir David Cuthbertson as President of the International Union of Nutritional Sciences was explaining to the Royal Society of London that nutrition was a science of great merit in its own right.'[52] However, by the early 1960s the study of food and its effect on health had diversified into several fields, which included the study of cancer-causing substances, micronutrients, dietetics and food technology. This diversification made it practically impossible for a new generation of researchers to continue the kind of wide-ranging, applied research that Muriel had carried out under the umbrella of nutritional science.

Although Muriel remained as director of the NRU until 1964, staying on past the official retirement age by invitation of the NZMRC, the closure of the unit was devastating to her. She became withdrawn and severely depressed. The dean of the Otago Medical School wrote: 'I am very concerned about Dr Muriel Bell who is resentful and in a state of acute depression.'[53] She preferred to work in isolation, despite the efforts of her close friends and colleagues to ensure that she continued to be recognised as a national expert in nutrition. To acknowledge Muriel's contribution, the NRC observed a minute of appreciation at its final meeting in February 1964: 'The outstanding feature of Dr Bell's Directorship of the Unit has been the spirit of dedication which she has displayed, never sparing herself when the need demanded, and indeed using every moment of her leisure in furthering the interests of her Department and developing the researches for which she had made herself responsible.'[54]

A scientist through and through

A number of organisations with which Muriel had been associated jointly hosted a luncheon in her honour in Wellington in March 1964. They included the Home Science Alumnae Association, the Health Department, the Plunket Society, and the Wheat Research Institute. Elizabeth Gregory, by then retired from her position as professor of home science, spoke of the cooperation between home science and nutrition researchers in educating teachers, dieticians and housewives, especially during the war. The minister of health, Don McKay, highlighted Muriel's work on iodised salt, school milk and water fluoridation as her main contributions to improving public health in New Zealand. Plunket's medical advisor, Neil Begg, praised her 'soundly balanced scientific judgement' on matters pertaining to infant health.[55] E.W. Hullett of the Wheat Research Institute applauded her efforts in 'straightening out the cranks and faddists in respect of flour and bread'. Charles Burns portrayed another, less combative side of Muriel: he spoke of 'the deep humanity … in her concern for the better nutrition of women and children … [and] the remarkable sense of dedication which placed her always at beck and call, and of her unselfish concern for those working with and for her'. These tributes gave Muriel a well-deserved farewell from public service, but they could not restore what had been taken from her. She might have felt some sense of relief at the decrease in her workload if she had not spent what must have seemed a lifetime building up the capacity of the Nutrition Research Unit for the benefit of the nation.

After her retirement, the accolades continued to come in. The highlight was the conferral of an honorary doctorate of science by the University of Otago in 1968. The orator, Professor Alan Horsman, described her as 'a tireless and peerless lady'.[56] For this occasion Muriel for once chose to dress up, buying a new blue suit. In recognition of her important work, the Human Nutrition Department at Otago University (established in 1971) founded a Muriel Bell Memorial Prize in Human Nutrition and a Muriel

Bell Memorial Lecture. Another permanent memorial to Muriel's career is a sundial in the rose garden at Wakari Hospital, donated by her friend and medical school classmate Frances Preston.

Ironically, Muriel's choice to restrict her research to fields that had the greatest potential to improve the well-being of New Zealanders, rather than pursuing the latest trends, gave her competitors an opportunity to oust her by labelling her science as old fashioned rather than cutting edge. Yet the expertise, dedication and passion she displayed in her fifteen years as director at the NRU were an inspiration for a generation of women in science. Colleagues spoke of her 'unparalleled devotion' and said simply, 'There will never be another.'[57]

In an interview with the historian Philippa Mein Smith, Marion Robinson revealed Muriel's last undertaking as a nutrition researcher. Left on her typewriter before she died was a finished article on the toxicity of the karaka berry, a project she had begun in the 1930s.[58] The article was published posthumously in the *New Zealand Journal of Science*.[59]

Muriel's return to this project invites comment. Having lost her workplace, she was left out on a limb. Fortunately, one of the few remaining privileges of her fifty-year association with Otago Medical School was access to the medical school building after hours, thanks to the sympathetic night porter, to use the former nutrition research laboratory. She developed peculiar working habits that caused concern among her friends and colleagues. One colleague recalled her working during the night in the laboratory after everyone else had gone home, and then being found asleep in her car the following morning. Why did she pursue the project? Perhaps she simply sought the satisfaction of seeing a task through to completion. But it is also possible that she saw this investigation into a uniquely New Zealand food, in the interests of the well-being of New Zealanders, as epitomising her career as a New Zealand nutrition researcher.

On 2 May 1974 Muriel was discovered dead in her home. Having been unable to contact Muriel for days, her stepsister Jean Williams feared for her well-being and called the police to break into Muriel's home. According to her, Muriel had choked on her own vomit and died. Williams had said, 'What a tragic end to a wonderful life.' Jean Williams recalled the police being 'very questioning really and asked me all sorts of details … The police doctor was horrible; the policemen themselves were marvellous.'[60] As a qualified doctor, Muriel had treated her own ailments over the years, so no known pre-existing condition could be identified as an obvious cause for her sudden death. An inquest was required.

The coroner's report stated gastroenteritis as the cause. However, Muriel's niece Mona Randall gave a different account. Although she cautioned that 'Muriel would turn in her grave if she knew I were telling you this', she said that Jean Williams had told her in confidence that Muriel had taken her own life.[61] If this is true, it is even more tragic that she was not able to prevent her own suffering in doing so.

If Muriel indeed took her own life, she apparently left no letter or note explaining her decision, so it is only possible to speculate on her reasons. The loss of her family, home, social milieu, daily routines and capacity for work might well have been among them. After Alf Hefford's death in 1957, she lived alone. Her sisters Elsie and Chris died in 1972. In the same year, on the advice of family and friends, Muriel moved into a flat. With this shift, she lost more than her St Clair home with its large garden and orchard: she lost a place filled with memories of her life in Dunedin since the late 1930s. She never settled in: when she died, most of her belongings were still in boxes.

Moreover, an inability to work would have deprived her of what mattered most to her. Muriel's life and work were intimately interwoven, and her personal life always came second to her professional role. The closure of the NRU left a gaping hole in her existence, and her colleagues' comments about its emotional effect on her suggest that demoralisation and depression may have played a part in a decision to end her life.

Muriel's loathing of wedding and funerals was well known, and she had made it clear that she wanted no funeral service. She was privately cremated in Dunedin on 4 May 1974, after which her ashes were sent to the cemetery in Nelson. Yet her stepsister Jean felt she could not allow Muriel's death to go unobserved, so, against her wishes, friends and family paid a final tribute to Muriel at a large memorial service in Andersons Bay, Dunedin.

The legacy of Muriel Bell

Current topics in nutrition research bear a striking resemblance to the range of projects that occupied Muriel Bell during her career: the role of calcium deficiency in osteoporosis, iodine deficiency diseases and an increase in vitamin D deficiency remind us that malnutrition and nutritional deficiencies are still of serious concern. But malnutrition in the form of nutritional excess is now the greatest concern from a public health perspective.

The rapid rise of obesity and related diseases, including diabetes, high blood pressure, cardiovascular disease, stroke and certain cancers, is one of the greatest public health challenges in New Zealand today. Everyday food choices based on ease and convenience, rather than nutritional balance, have contributed to this trend. The combination of a high-calorie diet, an inactive lifestyle and stress can be fatal. As in past centuries, a high correlation has been demonstrated between poverty and poor health outcomes in the twenty-first century, but now the relationship between food consumption and malnutrition is inverted: the number of calories consumed is too high.

The rise in childhood obesity is the single most alarming public health development of recent decades, and one that government has so far done little to address. It raises similar questions to those of the 1930s about the affordability and availability of essential foods for a healthy diet.

The simplistic tendency to demonise certain foods, such as saturated fats and refined sugars, fails to address misconceptions about healthy eating. If Muriel Bell were alive today, rather than condemning specific foods or ingredients she might draw on multidisciplinary expertise to examine the role each substance plays in the functioning of the body. She might consider the role of sugars in the diet as a whole, both as a significant source of energy and as contributors to diseases like obesity and diabetes. And, indeed, a positive trend in nutrition research is its recent synergy with other fields of study to consider diet in the context of other factors such as physical activity, family history and mental health.

Muriel Bell might be dismayed to observe the persistence of vitamin, mineral and micronutrient deficiencies. The terms 'goitre' and 'dental caries' have been superseded by 'thyroid disease' and 'tooth decay', but the conditions remain, along with dietary iodine deficiencies and a continuing public debate on water fluoridation, which is still opposed by a vocal minority of citizens.

Muriel might also have involved herself in addressing the modern challenge of vitamin D deficiency in New Zealand, a condition that has now been associated not only with rickets, as Muriel was aware early in her career, but also with cardiovascular disease, cancer and cognitive impairment. Our bodies can produce ample vitamin D given sufficient exposure to sunlight; but today such exposure is strongly discouraged by public health experts because of the risk of melanoma. Although in some other countries foods such as milk are supplemented with vitamin D, this is not the practice in New Zealand. Compounding the risk of vitamin D deficiency, obesity can impair the body's absorption of this vitamin.

Muriel's concerns about the health of women and children, and the challenges faced by family members or caregivers who bear the primary responsibility for buying and preparing healthy foods for a household, are as relevant as ever. Fundamental questions persist about what constitutes a healthy diet, and the government's role in making healthy foods both affordable and available to all New Zealanders. A recent return to concerns about nutrition during pregnancy, breastfeeding and early childhood also shows the enduring importance of her early concerns.

As Muriel understood, nutrition is a cornerstone of individual and public health. Nutrition researchers, nutritionists and dieticians have a vital role in shaping the health of New Zealand.

NOTES

INTRODUCTION

1. C.H. Fagge to J. Edwards, 9 July 1932, William Gibson Research Committee Correspondence, 1926–1932, M10, Royal Society of Medicine Archives, London.
2. Don Beaven, personal communication, 15 April 2005.
3. Jean Caradus Williams, interview with author, 16 April 2005.

CHAPTER ONE: A PIONEERING SPIRIT

1. Undated interview, Transcript of interviews with Dr Bell, MS-1078/003, Dr Muriel Bell: Papers, Hocken Collections Uare Taoka o Hākena, University of Otago.
2. 'New Zealand sheat family has strong link with damaged Somerset Church', *New Zealand Free Lance*, 30 July 1952.
3. Suzanne Aufricht, unpublished memoir.
4. Jean Caradus Williams, 'The Bell Family Affair', unpublished manuscript, iv.
5. Williams, 'The Bell Family Affair', v.
6. *Examiner*, 12 May 1864, cited in 'William Gordon Bell', V.R. Gunn Manuscript, MS Papers 01120–9, Alexander Turnbull Library; see also E.J. Wakefield, *Adventure in New Zealand* (London: John Murray, 1845; repr., 1908) 343.
7. J.N.W. Newport, *Footprints: The story of the settlement and development of the Nelson back country districts* (Christchurch: Whitcombe and Tombs Ltd, 1962), 152–53.
8. Muriel E. Bell, 'No. 271, How things began', Correspondence and clippings relating to Dr Bell's New Zealand *Listener* articles, MS-1078/063, Dr Muriel Bell: Papers.
9. Williams, 'The Bell Family Affair', vii.
10. Jim McAloon, *Nelson: A regional history* (Whatamango Bay: Cape Catley, 1997), 128.
11. D.C. Low, *Salute to the Scalpel: A medical history of the Nelson Province* (Nelson: D. Low, 1960).
12. Wallace Bell and Jean Williams, 'The environment into which Muriel Bell was born', unpublished manuscript, Rex Malthus, personal collection, 4.
13. Ibid., 3.
14. Margaret C. Brown, *Difficult Country: An informal history on Murchison* ([Murchison]: Murchison Historical & Museum Society, 1976), 127.
15. D.A. Hamer, ed., *The Webbs in New Zealand, 1898* (Wellington: Price Milburn, 1975), 55.

16. *Nelson Evening Mail*, 14 May 1917.
17. *Buller Post*, 18 March 1902.
18. *Nelson Evening Mail*, 14 May 1917.
19. 'Methodism in Murchison', unpublished paper, Murchison Museum Historical Society, 4.
20. Jean Caradus Williams, interview with author, 16 April 2005.
21. Bell and Williams, 'Environment', 2.
22. Brown, *Difficult Country*, 128.
23. Undated interview, Transcript of interviews with Dr Bell, MS-1078/003.
24. Muriel E. Bell, 'No. 11: How likes and dislikes for foods arrive', Correspondence and clippings relating to Dr Bell's New Zealand *Listener* articles, MS-1078/063.
25. 'Nutritionist revisits Nelson', *Nelson Evening Mail*, 12 March 1966.
26. Brown, *Difficult Country*, 156.
27. See, for example, an article in the WCTU's magazine: Luther Gulick, 'The Home Maker: What she ought to know', *White Ribbon*, 11 January 1900.
28. Bell and Williams, 'Environment', 6.
29. Undated newspaper cutting, Bunting's Scrapbook, 1903–8, Murchison Museum & Historical Society. This is a collection of clippings relating to Murchison in the 1900s.
30. Bell and Williams, 'Environment', 7.
31. Surgery was 'apparently' not attempted on Frank Bell (Bell and Williams, 'Environment', 7. The *Buller Post*'s account differs on this point, and I have taken the newspaper account as correct.
32. Jean Caradus Williams, *Slate Pencil to Word-Processor* (Christchurch: Waverley Press, 1995), 3.
33. Bell and Williams, 'Environment', 7.
34. Ibid.
35. Myrtle Randerson to a friend in Nelson, 1974, cited in Bell and Williams, 'Environment', 7.
36. Mona Randall, interview with author, 9 August 2005.
37. *Buller Post*, n.d., Bunting's Scrapbook, 1903–8; Bell and Williams, 'Environment', 7.
38. 'Terrible tramway accident. Mr & Mrs Thomas Bell the victims. Mrs Bell killed outright', 4 May 1907, Bunting's Scrapbook, 1903–8.
39. 'For your tram memories scrap book, curator of colonial history's account', *Evening Post*, n.d.
40. *Buller Post*, 7 May 1907.
41. Undated clipping, Bunting's Scrapbook, 1903–8.
42. *Nelson Evening Mail*, 14 May 1917.
43. Williams interview, 16 April 2005.
44. Bell and Williams, 'Environment', 8.
45. *Buller Post*, 29 October 1907.
46. Williams, *Slate Pencil to Word-Processor*, 4.

47. There is no record of domestic help in the two years before Thomas Bell's remarriage.
48. Undated interview, Transcript of interviews with Dr Bell, MS-1078/003.
49. Ibid.
50. 'Nutritionist revisits Nelson'.
51. Ibid.
52. Bell and Williams, 'Environment', 9.
53. Bell, 'No. 11: How Likes and Dislikes for Foods Arrive'.
54. *Nelson College for Girls: Fifty years, 1883–1933,* compiled by C.B. Mills and edited by the Jubilee Committee (Nelson: A.G. Betts, 1933), 86.
55. *Nelson College for Girls: Fifty years,* 86.
56. Ibid.
57. Undated interview, Transcript of interviews with Dr Bell, MS-1078/003.
58. *Nelson College for Girls: Fifty years*, 88.
59. 'Leslie George Bell, 1892–1963', *The Bell Family Affair*, newsletter no. 29, August 2003.
60. Bell and Williams, 'Environment', 10.
61. Undated interview, Transcript of interviews with Dr Bell, MS-1078/003.

CHAPTER TWO: MEDICINE AS A CAREER PATH

1. Marion F. Robinson, 'Muriel Emma Bell: Scientist and woman', in *The Moonstone: More about selenium; The First Muriel Bell Memorial Lecture* (Palmerston North: Nutrition Society of New Zealand, 1975), 9.
2. Carol Dyhouse, 'Driving ambitions: Women in pursuit of a medical education, 1890–1939', *Women's History Review 7*, no. 3, 1998, 321–41.
3. Daniel Colquhoun, 'On some realities: Terrible and otherwise. A plea for the Empire Service League', *Otago University Review 32*, no. 2, October 1918, 33. The Dunedin branch of the Empire Service League was established in 1918.
4. Derek A. Dow, *Safeguarding the Public Health: A history of the New Zealand Department of Health* (Wellington: Victoria University Press, 1995), 108.
5. Betty Tunnicliffe, 'Food, fresh air and cod liver oil', *In Our Lifetimes: A collection of reminiscences* (Rotorua: Rotorua Writers Group, 2001), 68–69.
6. Erik Olssen, 'Truby King and the Plunket Society: An analysis of a prescriptive ideology', *New Zealand Journal of History 15*, no. 1, 1981, 32–20.
7. Rima D. Apple, *Mothers and Medicine: A social history of infant feeding, 1890–1950* (Madison: University of Wisconsin Press, 1987), 131.
8. Linda Bryder, *A Voice for Mothers: The Plunket Society and infant welfare, 1907–2000* (Auckland: Auckland University Press, 2003), 80.
9. Dorothy Page, 'Dissecting a community: Women medical students at the University of Otago, 1891–1924', in *Communities of Women: Historical perspectives*, ed. Barbara Brookes and Dorothy Page (Dunedin: University of Otago Press, 2002), 115.

10. Obituary of Thomas Bell, *Nelson Evening Mail*, 14 May 1917.
11. Wallace Bell and Jean Williams, 'The environment into which Muriel Bell was born', Rex Malthus, personal collection, 10.
12. Bell and Williams, 'Environment', 11.
13. Mona Randall, interview with author, 9 August 2005.
14. 'Obituary: Dr Raynor Colin Bell', *New Zealand Dental Journal 21*, 1926, 227–28.
15. Kathleen Bell, interview with Marcy Varnham, 21 March 1993, Woodford House oral history project, Oral History Collection 0061, Alexander Turnbull Library, Wellington.
16. Kathleen Bell interview.
17. The student Christian Union took up the new ideals of the international Labour movement and concerned itself with moral education. See *The Australian Intercollegian 21*, 1918.
18. *Otago University Review 32*, no. 2, October 1918, 33.
19. *Otago University Review 33*, no. 1, June 1920, 68.
20. Nancy M. Taylor, *The New Zealand People at War*, vol. 1, *The Home Front*, (Wellington: Department of Internal Affairs, Historical Publications Branch, 1986), 171.
21. Page, 'Dissecting a community', 127.
22. Jubilee Records, '50 Years anniversary of the college (1961)', St Margaret's College: Records, AG-157 R, Hocken Collections Uare Taoka o Hākena, University of Otago.
23. Untitled newspaper clipping, *Otago Daily Times*, 4 September 1961.
24. Ibid.
25. George D. Sayer, quoted in Ann Strong, 'Home Science', *Otago University Review 35*, no. 2, October 1922, 29.
26. *Otago University Review 34*, no. 1, September 1921, 65.
27. Frances I. Preston, *Lady Doctor, Vintage Model* (Wellington: A.H. & A.W. Reed, 1974), 16.
28. Minutes of the November 1920 General Meeting, Women's Club General Meetings Minute Book 1915–22, MS 641 47/3, Hocken Collections Uare Taoka o Hākena, University of Otago.
29. Ibid.
30. Minutes of Meeting, 30 June 1920, Otago University Students' Association, Otago University Women's Club, Committee Meetings, Minute Book 1915–1922, MS 641 47/1, Hocken Collections Uare Taoka o Hākena, University of Otago.
31. Undated interview, Transcript of interviews with Dr Bell, MS-1078/003, Dr Muriel Bell: Papers, Hocken Collections Uare Taoka o Hākena, University of Otago.
32. Preston, *Lady Doctor*, 12.
33. Ibid., 41.
34. 'A woman's place: Medical student not wanted', *Otago Daily Times*, 11 August 1969.

35. Untitled article, notes of IFUW annual meeting in May 1922, *Otago University Review 35*, no. 2, October 1922, 58.
36. For an account of the medical curriculum and training, see Preston, *Lady Doctor,* 9–46.
37. Preston, *Lady Doctor,* 10.
38. Muriel E. Bell, 'John Malcolm: Obituary', *New Zealand Medical Journal 53*, no. 296, 1954, 436–39 ; James R. Robinson, 'Physiology', *Medical Research in Otago, 1922–1997: As portrayed by 75 years of the proceedings of the University of Otago Medical School* (Dunedin: Otago Medical School Research Society, 1998), 59.
39. John Malcolm to Edward Schaefer, 24 February 1913, in Taylor, Douglass William, Professor: Letters, 1905–1932, from Professor John Malcolm, Dunedin, to Sir Edward Sharpey-Schafer (1905–1932), Hocken Collections Uare Taoka o Hākena, University of Otago.
40. Gordon Bell and Charles Hercus, *Otago Medical School under the First Three Deans* (Edinburgh: E. & S. Livingstone Ltd, 1964), 186.
41. Douglas Robb, *Medical Odyssey* (Auckland: Collins, 1967), 25.
42. Ibid.
43. Bell and Hercus, *Otago Medical School,* 186.
44. Frank Fitchett, 'The Teaching of Pharmacology: A report by Professor Fitchett', in Bell and Hercus, *Otago Medical School,* 368.
45. Bell, 'Obituary: John Malcolm', 438.
46. Preston, *Lady Doctor,* 535–37.
47. Margaret D. Maxwell, compiler, *Women Doctors in New Zealand: An historical perspective, 1921–1986* (Auckland: IMS, 1990), 124.
48. Preston, *Lady Doctor,* 54.

CHAPTER THREE: RESEARCH

1. Michael Belgrave, 'A subtle containment: Women in New Zealand medicine, 1893–1941', *New Zealand Journal of History 22*, no. 1, April 1988, 44–55. See also R.E. Wright-St Clair, 'Women in New Zealand medicine before 1930', in Margaret D. Maxwell, *Women Doctors in New Zealand : An historical perspective, 1921–1986* (Auckland: IMS, 1990), 163–79.
2. One such meeting of seven medical women took place on 27 October 1921, with Dr Emily Siedeberg, Winifred Bathgate, Marion Whyte, Grace Stevenson, Emma Irwin, Emily Nees and Ina Moody in attendance. The Medical Women's Association was established on 19 December 1921. See Maxwell, *Women Doctors in New Zealand,* 1.
3. 'Annual report of Dunedin Branch of New Zealand Medical Women's Association', *New Zealand Medical Journal 27*, 1928, 180.
4. Lady Florence Barrett, 'President's foreword', *Medical Women's International Journal 1*, no. 2, November 1925, 3.
5. Barrett, 'President's foreword', 4.

6. Janet C. Angus, *By Degrees: The history of the Otago Branch of the New Zealand Federation of University Women, 1921–83* (Dunedin: New Zealand Federation of University Women, Otago Branch, 1984), 121–23.
7. Gordon Bell and Charles Hercus, *Otago Medical School under the First Three Deans* (Edinburgh: E. & S. Livingstone Ltd, 1964), 233.
8. Undated interview, Transcript of interviews with Dr Bell, MS-1078/003, Dr Muriel Bell: Papers, Hocken Collections Uare Taoka o Hākena, University of Otago.
9. Ibid.
10. Charles Burns, *Some Aspects of Alcohol Use and Human Nutrition, with Special Reference to the Acute Alcohol Withdrawal Syndrome*, Third Muriel Bell Memorial Lecture, 10 February 1977 (Palmerston North: Nutrition Society of New Zealand, 1977), 1.
11. Undated interview, Transcript of interviews with Dr Bell, MS-1078/003.
12. Ibid.
13. Muriel E. Bell, 'Nutrition in New Zealand: Forty years' history, 1920–1960', *Supplement to the Journal of the New Zealand Association of Home Science Alumnae (N.Z.) 31*, 1962, 28.
14. Undated interview, Transcript of interviews with Dr Bell, MS-1078/003.
15. Muriel E. Bell, 'Mineral deficiencies in New Zealand', *Journal of the American Dental Association 40*, no. 3, 1962, 20–42.
16. Diana Brown, '"Stepping-stone to cretinism": Goitre in New Zealand, 1920–1950', B.A. (Hons) research essay, University of Otago, 2000.
17. Frances I. Preston, *Lady Doctor, Vintage Model* (Wellington: A.H. & A.W. Reed, 1974), 57.
18. Muriel E. Bell, *Some Studies in Basal Metabolism* (Wellington: Wellington Publishing Company Ltd, 1923). Also published in *New Zealand Medical Journal 22*, 1923, 322–32.
19. Ibid., 3.
20. Burns, *Some Aspects of Alcohol Use and Human Nutrition,* 2.
21. Undated interview, Transcript of interviews with Dr Bell, MS-1078/003.
22. Wallace Bell and Jean Williams, 'The environment into which Muriel Bell was born', Rex Malthus, personal collection.
23. Preston, *Lady Doctor,* 55.
24. Muriel E. Bell, 'Danger in raw milk', *Listener,* 27 November 1950.
25. Barbara Smith, interview with author, 12 April 2005.
26. Burns, *Some Aspects of Alcohol Use and Human Nutrition,* 1.
27. Douglas Robb, *Medical Odyssey* (Auckland: Collins, 1967), 31.
28. *Otago Witness,* 3 August 1926, 45.
29. Maxwell, *Women Doctors in New Zealand,* 1–3.
30. John Malcolm to Lindo Ferguson, 14 July 1926, Correspondence relating to Muriel Bell's MD examination, MS-2640/030, Malcolm Family Papers: Papers particularly relating to Professor John Malcolm, Hocken Collections Uare Taoka o Hākena, University of Otago.

31. Norman Edson, Typescript of reminiscences of the Physiology and Biochemistry Departments, MS 1623/023, University of Otago Medical Library: Historical Collection, Hocken Collections Uare Taoka o Hākena, University of Otago.
32. C.R. Burns, 'Postgraduate study', *Digest of the Otago University Medical Students Association 1*, no. 1 (October 1934), 35.
33. 'Post-graduate research, Great Britain', *Medical Women's International Journal 1*, no. 2, November 1925, 67.
34. Paul Baker, *King and Country Call: New Zealanders, conscription and the Great War* (Auckland: Auckland University Press, 1988), 178; Archibald Baxter, *We Will Not Cease* (Auckland: Penguin, 1987).
35. Jocelyn Harris, personal communication, 12 April 2005.
36. Betty Holt, *Women for Peace and Freedom: A history of the Women's International League for Peace and Freedom in New Zealand* (Wellington: Women's International League for Peace and Freedom, 1985), 15.
37. Jean Caradus Williams, interview with author, 16 April 2005.
38. Millicent Amiel Baxter, *The Memoirs of Millicent Baxter* (Whatamongo Bay: Cape Catley, 1981), 66.
39. Jim Hefford, interview with author, Wellington, 13 May 2005.
40. Brigid Pike, 'Jean Park, Hetty Weitzel', in *Book of New Zealand Women: Ko kui ma te kaupapa,* ed. Charlotte Macdonald, Merimeri Penfold and Bridget Williams (Wellington: Bridget Williams Books, 1991), 497–500; Edson, Typescript of reminiscences.
41. 'Annual Report of Dunedin Branch of New Zealand Medical Women's Association', 180.
42. Burns, *Some Aspects of Alcohol Use and Human Nutrition,* 2.

CHAPTER FOUR: KNOWING BY INSTINCT

1. 'Post graduate study in Vienna', *New Zealand Medical Journal 31*, 1932, 383–89.
2. Muriel E. Bell, 'No. 187: Our minerals', Correspondence and clippings relating to Dr Bell's New Zealand *Listener* articles, MS-1078/063, Dr Muriel Bell: Papers, Hocken Collections Uare Taoka o Hākena, University of Otago.
3. Margaret D. Maxwell, compiler, *Women Doctors in New Zealand: An historical perspective, 1921–1986* (Auckland: IMS, 1990), 76.
4. *Medical Women's International Journal 1*, no. 6 (May 1928).
5. Muriel E. Bell, 'School milk', Milk in Schools, MS-1078/001, Dr Muriel Bell: Papers.
6. Maxwell, *Women Doctors in New Zealand,* 4.
7. Carol Dyhouse, 'Women students and the London medical schools, 1914–39: The anatomy of a masculine culture', *Gender and History 10*, no. 1, April 1998, 110–32.
8. Muriel E. Bell to J. Edwards, 28 July 1929, William Gibson Research Committee,

Correspondence 1926–1932, M10, Royal Society of Medicine Archives, London.
9. Robin Hyde, Gill Boddy and Jacqueline Matthews, *Disputed Ground: Robin Hyde, journalist* (Wellington: Victoria University Press, 1991), 147.
10. Minutes, 1 July 1929, William Gibson Research Committee Minute Book 1919–57, M7, Royal Society of Medicine Archives, London.
11. Undated interview, Transcript of interviews with Dr Bell, MS-1078/003, Dr Muriel Bell: Papers.
12. Ernest Marsden to Muriel E. Bell, 3 September 1929, William Gibson Research Committee, Correspondence 1926–1932, M10, Royal Society of Medicine Archives, London.
13. Muriel E. Bell to J. Edwards, 7 September 1929, William Gibson Research Committee Correspondence, 1926–1932, M10.
14. Undated interview, Transcript of interviews with Dr Bell, MS-1078/003.
15. Muriel E. Bell, 'Mineral deficiencies in New Zealand', *Journal of the American Dental Association 40*, no. 3, 1962, 204.
16. Muriel E. Bell, 'Report to Royal Society of Medicine', 9 July 1930, William Gibson Research Committee, Minute Book 1919–1957, M7, Royal Society of Medicine Archives, London.
17. Bell, 'Report to Royal Society of Medicine'.
18. Undated interview, Transcript of interviews with Dr Bell, MS-1078/003.
19. Muriel E. Bell, 'Nutrition unit – letters to the editor', *Evening Star*, 11 September, 1963.
20. Tom Jaine, 'Introduction', in J.C. Drummond and Anne Wilbraham, *The Englishman's Food: A history of five centuries of English diet* (1957; repr., London: Pimlico, 1991), 9–10.
21. Alice M. Copping, 'Sir Jack Cecil Drummond, F.R.S: A biographical sketch', *Journal of Nutrition 82*, no. 1, January 1964, 5.
22. Elizabeth McLaughlin, 'Dr Elizabeth Gregory', *Newsletter of the Association of Home Science Alumnae,* March 1984, 2.
23. McLaughlin, 'Dr Elizabeth Gregory'.
24. Undated interview transcript, Biographical information on Dr Bell and notes relating to nutrition, MS-1078/108, Dr Muriel Bell: Papers.
25. Undated interview, Transcript of interviews with Dr Bell, MS-1078/003.
26. Muriel E. Bell, 'Report to Council awarding William Gibson Research Scholarship', 31 December 1930, William Gibson Research Committee, Minute Book 1919–1957, M7.
27. Arini Fisher to John Malcolm, 23 January 1932, MS-2640/009, Malcolm Family Papers, Papers particularly relating to Professor Malcolm, Hocken Collections Uare Taoka o Hākena, University of Otago.
28. *Dietetics: A course of lectures delivered at University College Hospital,* supplement to *University College Hospital Magazine* (London: John Bale, 1930).
29. Maxwell, *Women Doctors in New Zealand,* 77, incorrectly states that the conference was held in Vienna.

30. 'Imperial Social Hygiene Congress', *British Medical Journal 2*, July 1931, 157.
31. C.H. Fagge to J. Edwards, 9 July 1932, William Gibson Research Committee Correspondence, 1926–1932, M10.
32. Muriel E. Bell, Elizabeth Gregory and J.C. Drummond, 'Studies of the alleged toxic action of cod liver oil and concentrates of vitamin A', *Zeitschrift für Vitaminforschung* 2, no. 3, July 1933, 161–82; Muriel E. Bell, 'Albuminuria in the normal male rat', *Journal of Physiology 79*, no. 2, 1933, 191–93; Muriel Emma Bell, 'High protein diets and acid-base mechanism', *Biochemical Journal 27*, no. 5, 1933, 1430–37; Muriel Emma Bell, 'Cystine and nephrotoxicity', *Biochemical Journal 27*, no. 4, 1933, 1267–70.
33. Charles Burns, *Some Aspects of Alcohol Use and Human Nutrition, with Special Reference to the Acute Alcohol Withdrawal Syndrome: Third Muriel Bell Memorial Lecture*, 10 February 1977 (Palmerston North: Nutrition Society of New Zealand, 1977), 2.
34. Esme R. Turner, 'Dr Muriel E. Bell, M.D. (NZ)', *Woman Today,* March 1938, 270–71.
35. M.M. Campbell to H.E. Holland, 16 October 1927, Correspondence 1903–1931, MS-Papers 1815-02, H.E. Holland, Alexander Turnbull Library, Wellington.
36. Gary Werskey, *The Visible College: A collective biography of British socialists and scientists of the 1930s* (London: Allen Lane, 1978), 25.
37. Jim Saunders, undated postcard, Rex Malthus, personal collection.
38. Aldous Huxley, ed., *An Encyclopaedia of Pacifism* (London: Chatto & Windus, 1937), 40.
39. Naomi Black, 'The mothers' International: The Women's Co-operative Guild and feminist pacifism', *Women's Studies International Forum 7*, no. 6, 1984, 467–76.
40. Fisher to Malcolm, 23 January 1932.
41. Undated interview, Transcript of interviews with Dr Bell, MS-1078/003.
42. Muriel E. Bell, 'A case of chylothorax', *British Medical Journal 1*, 1935, 1211–16.
43. Frances I. Preston, *Lady Doctor, Vintage Model* (Wellington: A.H. & A.W. Reed, 1974), 56.
44. Bernard Harris, 'Government and charity in the distressed mining areas of England and Wales, 1928–30', in *Medicine and Charity before the Welfare State,* ed. Jonathan Barry and Colin Jones (London: Routledge, 1991), 207–24.
45. Elizabeth Peretz, 'The costs of modern motherhood to low income families in interwar Britain', in *Women and Children First: International maternal and infant welfare, 1870–1945,* ed. Valerie Fildes, Lara V. Marks and Hilary Marland (London; New York: Routledge, 1992), 263.
46. A.M.N. Pringle, 'An enquiry into malnutrition', 1938, cited in Fildes, Marks and Marland, *Women and Children First,* 279n18.
47. Malcolm McKinnon, *The Broken Decade: Prosperity, depression and recovery in New Zealand, 1928–1939* (Dunedin: Otago University Press, 2016), 141.
48. Muriel E. Bell, 'No. 238, Nutritional wedding', Correspondence and clippings relating to Dr Bell's New Zealand *Listener* articles, MS-1078/063.

49. Tony Simpson, *The Sugarbag Years* (Auckland: Godwit, 1997), 190.
50. McKinnon, *The Broken Decade,* 171–72.
51. Muriel E. Bell, 'Submission to the Commission on Education by NZ Milk Board re: School Milk', undated, Milk in Schools, MS-1078/001.
52. 'Nutrition Classes and Health Camps', *New Zealand Official Yearbook, 1934* (Wellington: Government Printer, 1934), 137.
53. Derek A. Dow, *Safeguarding the Public Health: A history of the New Zealand Department of Health* (Wellington: Victoria University Press, 1995), 141.
54. D.G. McMillan, 'A National Health Service: New Zealand of to-morrow', *Digest of the Otago University Medical Students Association 1*, no. 1, October 1934, 28.

CHAPTER FIVE: GAINING GROUND IN NEW ZEALAND

1. Jim Hefford, personal communication, 22 April 2005.
2. Hilary Stance, 'Janet Fraser: Making policy as well as tea', in Margaret Clark, *Peter Fraser: Master politician* (Palmerston North: Dunmore Press, 1998), 64.
3. Michael Belgrave, 'Needs and the State: Evolving social policy in New Zealand history', in *Past Judgement: Social policy in New Zealand history,* ed. Bronwyn Dalley and Margaret Tennant (Dunedin: University of Otago Press, 2004), 23–26.
4. James Ng, *Windows on a Chinese Past* (Dunedin: Otago Heritage Books, 1999), vol. 3, 413.
5. League of Nations Health Organisation, resolution based on 1935 report 'Nutrition and public health', International Affairs Social Affairs Health Nutrition and Dietetics, EA2 1956/4b 108/7/67 1a, Department of External Affairs, National Archives, Wellington.
6. W.B. Sutch, *The Quest for Security in New Zealand* (Wellington: Oxford University Press, 1966), 242.
7. Margaret McClure, *A Civilised Community: A history of social security in New Zealand, 1898–1998* (Auckland: Auckland University Press, 1998), 80–81.
8. *New Zealand Medical Journal 36*, 1937, 349–51, cited in Derek Dow, 'Driving their own health canoe: Maori and health research', in *Past Judgement: Social policy in New Zealand history*, ed. Bronwyn Dalley and Margaret Tennant, (Dunedin: University of Otago Press, 2004), 95.
9. D.W. Carmalt-Jones, *Annals of the University of Otago Medical School, 1875–1939* (Wellington: A.H. & A.W Reed, 1945), 239; Gordon Bell and Charles Hercus, *Otago Medical School under the First Three Deans* (Edinburgh: E. & S. Livingstone Ltd, 1964), 233–34.
10. Bell and Hercus, *Otago Medical School*, 234.
11. Carmalt-Jones, *Annals,* 239.
12. Margaret Neave, interview with author, 14 May 2005.
13. Cited in Dorothy Page, *Anatomy of a Medical School: A history of medicine at the University of Otago, 1875–2000* (Dunedin: University of Otago Press, 2008), 90.

14. Sandys Wünsch to John Malcolm, 14 January 1936, Cobalt research and related papers, MS-1078/066, Dr Muriel Bell: Papers, Hocken Collections Uare Taoka o Hākena, University of Otago.
15. C.A. Elvehjem and F.J. Stare, 'Cobalt in animal nutrition', *Journal of Biological Chemistry 99*, 1933, 473.
16. J.K. Dixon to Muriel E. Bell, 23 January 1936, Cobalt research and related papers, MS-1078/066.
17. E.J. Underwood & J.F. Filmer, 'Enzootic marasmus: The determination of the biologically potent element (cobalt) in limonite', *Australian Veterinary Journal 11*, 1935, 84–92.
18. J.K. Dixon to Muriel E. Bell, 18 November 1936, Cobalt research and related papers, MS-1078/066. See also Muriel E. Bell, 'Some physiological aspects of the cobalt problem', *New Zealand Journal of Science and Technology 18*, 1937, 716–19.
19. Undated interview transcript, Biographical information on Dr Bell and notes relating to nutrition, MS-1078/108, Dr Muriel Bell: Papers.
20. E.R. Turner, 'Muriel E. Bell, M.D.', *Woman Today*, March 1938, 270–71.
21. Muriel E. Bell, 'Correspondence: Health of children', *Woman Today*, March 1938, 288.
22. 'Welfare centres', *Woman Today*, May 1938, 47.
23. Turner, 'Muriel E. Bell, M.D.'
24. Margaret D. Maxwell, *Women Doctors in New Zealand: An historical perspective, 1921–1986* (Auckland: IMS, 1990), 7.
25. Janet C. Angus, *By Degrees: The history of the Otago Branch of the New Zealand Federation of University Women, 1921–83* (Dunedin: New Zealand Federation of University Women, Otago Branch, 1984) 37.
26. Editorial Committee, Minutes of 22 February 1937 meeting, Minutes of Conferences & Committee Meetings of *Woman Today*, 3 December 1936–6 Nov 1939, Alexander Turnbull Library, Wellington.
27. Turner, 'Muriel E. Bell, M.D.'
28. Muriel E. Bell to Michael Watt, 1 October 1940, H 1 241 B130, Medical Research Council Nutrition Research, National Archives, Wellington.

CHAPTER SIX: STATE NUTRITIONIST DURING WORLD WAR II

1. *New Zealand Parliamentary Debate 252*, August 1938, 468, cited in Derek Dow, 'Driving their own health canoe: Maori and health research', in *Past Judgement: Social policy in New Zealand history*, ed. Bronwyn Dalley and Margaret Tennant, (Dunedin: University of Otago Press, 2004), 97.
2. NZMRC Minutes, 6 June 1944, Council Papers 1945, MS-1636/005, University of Otago Medical Library: Historical Collection, Hocken Collections Uare Taoka o Hākena, University of Otago.
3. Muriel E. Bell, 'John Malcolm, obituary', *New Zealand Medical Journal 53*, no.

296, 1954, 437.

4. Derek A. Dow, 'Hercus, Charles Ernest, 1888–1971', Dictionary of New Zealand Biography: www.teara.govt.nz/en/biographies/4h28/hercus-charles-ernest
5. Derek A. Dow, 'Watt, Michael Herbert, 1887–1967', Dictionary of New Zealand Biography: www.teara.govt.nz/en/biographies/4w8/watt-michael-herbert
6. Sir Charles Burns, 'Nutrition Society of New Zealand, Third Muriel Bell Memorial Lecture: Some aspects of alcohol use and human nutrition with special reference to the Acute Alcohol Withdrawal Syndrome, delivered 10 February 1977', *Proceedings of the Nutrition Society of New Zealand*, 1977, 27.
7. Ibid.
8. Gordon Bell and Charles Hercus, *Otago Medical School under the First Three Deans* (Edinburgh: E. & S. Livingstone Ltd, 1964) 180.
9. Norman Edson, Typescript of reminiscences of the Physiology and Biochemistry Departments, MS-1623/023, Hocken Collections Uare Taoka o Hākena, University of Otago.
10. Undated interview, Transcript of interviews with Dr Bell, MS-1078/003, Dr Muriel Bell: Papers, Hocken Collections Uare Taoka o Hākena, University of Otago.
11. 'Report of Nutrition Research Committee 1939–40', Report of Nutrition Research Committee dietary survey, MS-1078/009, Dr Muriel Bell: Papers.
12. Nutrition Research Committee of Medical Research Council, 'Report of Nutrition Research Committee of MRC for year ending March 31, 1939', MS-1078/089, Dr Muriel Bell: Papers.
13. 'Report: Suggestions for research work on nutrition submitted to MRC February at first meeting', Correspondence between Watt and Malcolm, MS-2798/009, Malcolm Family Papers, Hocken Collections Uare Taoka o Hākena, University of Otago.
14. 'Nutrition in Dominion: Investigation Plan approved, questionnaire on diet proposed, programme for medical research', *The Press,* 21 June 1938.
15. Malcolm McKinnon, *The Broken Decade: Prosperity, depression and recovery in New Zealand, 1928–1939* (Dunedin: Otago University Press, 2016), 266–67.
16. W.B. Sutch, 'Milk for schools: The government's scheme explained', *National Education 2*, December 1935, 502–03.
17. C.A.L. Treadwell, 'National milk scheme, children's health: Wellington's example, voluntary or state?' *Evening Post,* 9 August 1935.
18. H.C. Corry Mann, *Diets for Boys during the School Age*, Medical Research Council Special Report Series No. 105 (London: HMSO, 1926).
19. Muriel E. Bell, 'School milk in New Zealand, 14th International Dairy Congress', Milk in Schools, MS-1078/001, Dr Muriel Bell: Papers.
20. Department of Health, Division of School Hygiene, *Suggestions to Parents* [c. 1934], Milk for schools 1930–36, H 1 35/102 b.12, Department of Health, National Archives, Wellington.

21. League of Health of NZ Youth, 1935 pamphlet emphasising importance of milk for children and calling for national scheme, Milk for schools 1930–36, H 1 35/102 b.12.
22. Bell, 'School milk in New Zealand'.
23. 'Milk in schools: "Much unfounded talk about waste,"' *Otago Daily Times*, 24 June 1955.
24. 'Milk in schools: 230,000 children can't be wrong', *National Education 23*, October 1941, 340.
25. Sutch, 'Milk for schools', 502.
26. Minutes of the meeting of the Central Milk Council, 27–28 February 1945, Minutes Central Milk Council 1945–51, AATJ W4100 9 1, National Archives, Wellington.
27. Muriel E. Bell, 'Report of nutritionist for the year 1944–45', Nutrition reports, MS-1078/071, Dr Muriel Bell: Papers.
28. Ibid.
29. 'The case for pasteurisation', *New Zealand National Review,* 15 December 1944, 75.
30. Muriel E. Bell, 'Report of nutritionist for the year 1945–46', Nutrition reports, MS-1078/071.
31. F.H. McDowall, A.K. McDowell, J. Jean Clemow and Muriel E. Bell, 'The effect of sunlight on the nutritional properties and flavour of milk in glass bottles', Dr Bell's radio talks and articles, MS-1078/058, Dr Muriel Bell: Papers.
32. Muriel E. Bell to Doris Gordon, director of maternal welfare, Department of Health, 3 February 1947, Medical Research Nutrition 1946–50, YCBN 5977 60g 240/2, National Archives, Auckland.
33. Minutes of the meeting of the Central Milk Council, 5 March 1948, Minutes Central Milk Council 1945–51, AATJ W4100 9 1.
34. Ola Rudman, 'Seeing's believing', *New Zealand Women's Weekly,* 12 December 1946, 18.
35. Minutes of the meeting of the Central Milk Council, 17 October 1945, Minutes Central Milk Council 1945–51, AATJ W4100 9 1.
36. Muriel E. Bell, 'Report of the nutritionist for the year ending 31 March 1948', Nutrition reports, MS-1078/071.
37. Muriel E. Bell, 'No 118: First things first', Correspondence and clippings relating to Dr Bell's New Zealand *Listener* articles, MS-1078/063, Dr Muriel Bell: Papers.
38. Muriel E. Bell, 'Report of nutritionist for year 1948–49', Nutrition reports, MS-1078/071.
39. Muriel E. Bell, 'Notes on policies and performances of the Nutrition Research Department to 1957', Dr Muriel Bell, AG-0070-04/263, Royal New Zealand Plunket Society: Records, Hocken Collections Uare Taoka o Hākena, University of Otago.
40. Muriel E. Bell to Hilda Ross, 18 February 1952, Appointment Central Milk Council, 1945–53, ADOO 17021, IMD2 3/2, National Archives, Wellington.
41. Undated interview, Transcript of interviews with Dr Bell, MS-1078/003.

42. Sandra Coney, 'New Zealand Women's Food Value League, 1937–1948', in *Women Together: A history of women's organisations in New Zealand: Nga ropu wahine o te motu,* ed. Anne Else (Wellington: Department of Internal Affairs, 1993), 270–71; Sandra Coney, 'New Zealand Women's Food Value League', in *Standing in the Sunshine: A history of New Zealand women since they won the vote* (Auckland: Viking, 1993), 100–01.
43. Coney, 'New Zealand Women's Food Value League', 270–71.
44. 'Books in Brief: Modern food habits, [by] Guy Chapman', *New Zealand Women's Weekly*, 12 August 1937.
45. Editorial Committee, Minutes of 22 February 1937 meeting, Minutes of Conferences & Committee Meetings of *Woman Today,* 3 December 1936–6 November 1939, Alexander Turnbull Library, Wellington.
46. V. Macmillan, 'The home in the country: What A.C.E. does for the farmer's wife', *New Zealand Journal of Agriculture 58*, 1939, 51–54.
47. W.M. Stenhouse, *Whitcombe's Everyday Cookery for every Housewife: 1,067 copyright, selected, and tested recipes, revised by cooking experts and leading dieticians* (Christchurch: Whitcombe and Tombs, c. 1939), 6.
48. Vernon Henry Mottram, 'Food and the housewife', in J.C. Drummond, John Boyd Orr, Robert McCarrison et al., *The Nation's Larder and the Housewife's Part Therein* (London: G. Bell and Sons, 1940), 96.
49. Elizabeth Gregory and Elizabeth C.G. Wilson, *Good Nutrition*, ed. Muriel E. Bell on behalf of the Nutrition Research Committee of New Zealand Medical Research Council (Wellington: Department of Health, 1939, 1944 (wartime edition), repr. 1942, 1945, 1952, 1956).
50. Muriel E. Bell to R.A. Shore, acting director general of health, 4 June 1939, Medical Research Council Nutrition Research, H 1 241 B130, Department of Health, National Archives, Wellington.
51. On nurses, see *Kai Tiaki 38*, no. 6, June 1945, 131. On pharmacists, see Mr Clayton, secretary, Publicity Committee, Department of Health, to Muriel E. Bell, 2 October 1941, Health Education Publicity Work, Good Nutrition, General, 1941–49, H1 34/20, Department of Health, National Archives, Wellington.
52. Margaret Tennant, '"Missionaries of health": The School Medical Service during the inter-war period', in *A Healthy Country: Essays on the social history of medicine in New Zealand,* ed. Linda Bryder (Wellington: Bridget Williams Books, 1991), 146–47.
53. Ulric Williams to Michael Savage, 11 February 1938, cited in Derek Dow, *Safeguarding the Public Health: A history of the New Zealand Department of Health* (Wellington: Victoria University Press, 1995), 131.
54. Dow, *Safeguarding the Public Health,* 139.
55. 'Editorial: Vitamins', *New Zealand Medical Journal 37*, 1938, 184.
56. 'Report of Nutrition Committee of MRC for year ending March 31, 1939', Nutrition Committee of Medical Research Council, MS-1078/089, Hocken Collections Uare Taoka o Hākena, University of Otago.

57. Muriel E. Bell to Michael Watt, 8 June 1939, Medical Research Council Nutrition Research, H 1 241 B130.
58. Ibid.
59. Michael Watt to John Malcolm, 15 December 1939, Medical Research Council Nutrition Research, H 1 241 B130.
60. Muriel E. Bell to Michael Watt, 10 February 1940, Medical Research Council Nutrition Research, H 1 241 B130.
61. 'Report of Nutrition Research Committee 1939–1940', Report of Nutrition Research Committee dietary survey, MS-1078/009.
62. 'The Darkest Hour' speech, 30 May 1940, in House of Representatives, in *Selections from the Wartime Addresses of the Rt Hon Peter Fraser, Prime Minister of New Zealand* (Wellington: EV Paul Govt Printer, 1946), 12.
63. Jocelyn Harris, personal communication, 12 April 2005.
64. Report of Nutritional Research Committee dietary survey, MS-1078/009.
65. *The School Lunch* (Wellington: Government Printer, Department of Health, 1950); reissued as *School Lunches* (Wellington: Government Printer, Department of Health, 1953).
66. Muriel E. Bell, 'Report of nutrition officer 1940–41', Miscellaneous nutrition research reports and related correspondence, MS-1078/006, Dr Muriel Bell: Papers.
67. Muriel E. Bell to R.A. Shore, 25 December 1941, Health Education Publicity Work, Pamphlets and Booklets 1941–46, H1 34/9, National Archives, Wellington.
68. Muriel E. Bell, 'Preserve black currants', Correspondence and clippings relating to Dr Bell's New Zealand *Listener* articles, MS-1078/063.
69. Muriel E. Bell, 'No. 39: Gather ye rose hips while ye may', Correspondence and clippings relating to Dr Bell's New Zealand *Listener* articles, MS-1078/063.
70. Muriel E. Bell, 'No. 25: New Zealand grapefruit', Correspondence and clippings relating to Dr Bell's New Zealand *Listener* articles, MS-1078/063.
71. Bell, 'No. 39: Gather Ye Rose Hips While Ye May.'
72. Muriel E. Bell, 'Report of Nutrition Committee for year ending 31 March 1946', Nutrition reports, MS-1078/071.
73. Bell, 'Notes on policies and performances of the Nutrition Research Department to 1957'.
74. Bell, 'Report of Nutrition Committee for year ending 31 March 1946'.
75. Muriel E. Bell, 'Report on the commercial trial of higher extraction flour', Nutrition reports, MS-1078/071.
76. Bell, 'Notes on policies and performances of the Nutrition Research Department to 1957'.
77. Ibid.
78. Mona Randall, interview with author, 9 August 2005.
79. Jim Hefford, interview with author, 13 May 2005.

CHAPTER SEVEN: DRIVING DIETARY CHANGES FORWARD

1. Muriel E. Bell, 'Report of nutritionist for the year ending 31 March 1948', Nutrition reports, MS-1078/071, Dr Muriel Bell: Papers, Hocken Collections Uare Taoka o Hākena, University of Otago.
2. 'Presidential address to the Australian and New Zealand Association for the Advancement of Science, Canberra, 13th January 1954', in Theodore Rigg & ANZAAS, *Role of Science in the Development of New Zealand Agriculture* (Nelson: Cawthron Institute, 1954), 18.
3. 'Not vegetables but fat', *NZ Commerce,* May 1946.
4. Norma Metson, 'Spreading the food ration: World faces acute shortage', *New Zealand Journal of Agriculture 72*, January 1946, 103–05.
5. Muriel E. Bell, 'Sugar enough, if you study the uses of it: Three articles by Dr Muriel Bell', AG-0071–1/44, Royal New Zealand Plunket Society: Records, Hocken Collections Uare Taoka o Hākena, University of Otago.
6. 'Packing parcels for overseas', *New Zealand Journal of Agriculture 76*, April 1948, 406–08.
7. Jabberwocky, 'Gifts of fat are forging new links with Britain', *NZ Women's Weekly,* 3 February 1949, 10.
8. Frances Preston, Newsletter written by Frances Preston and papers relating to Fat for Britain campaign, December 1949, MS-2432/009, Preston Family Papers, Hocken Collections Uare Taoka o Hākena, University of Otago.
9. 'Public ill-health: Need for action', *NZ National Review,* 15 September 1945, 73.
10. Muriel E. Bell, *Nutrition in the First Five Years,* lectures given at a refresher course on the pre-school child to medical officers of the Department of Health, August 1948 (Wellington: R.E. Owen, 1949), 34.
11. 'Nutrition: National health requires adequate nutrition', *New Zealand Journal of Agriculture 74*, May 1947, 536.
12. Bell, *Nutrition in the First Five Years.*
13. 'One in 10 NZ children has a bad food habit', *Standard*, 3 October 1949; 'Malnutrition in NZ', *Auckland Star,* 9 July 1949.
14. Harold Turbott to minister of health, 22 June 1948, Nutrition General 1946–49, H 1 31, Department of Health, National Archives, Wellington.
15. *New Zealand Official Yearbook 1950* (Wellington: Government Printer, 1950), 827; *New Zealand Official Yearbook, 1934* (Wellington: Government Printer, 1934).
16. Muriel E. Bell to Miss McKenzie, dietician, 9 September 1948, Nutrition General 1946–49, H 1 31, Department of Health, National Archives, Wellington.
17. Muriel E. Bell, 'Mineral deficiencies in New Zealand', *Journal of the American Dental Association 40*, no. 3, 1962, 205.
18. Muriel E. Bell, 'Nutrition research: General speech', Dr Bell's radio talks and articles, MS-1078/058, Dr Muriel Bell: Papers.
19. Muriel E. Bell, 'Report of nutritionist 1942–43', Miscellaneous nutrition research reports and related correspondence, MS-1078/006, Dr Muriel Bell: Papers.

20. Ibid.
21. E.V. McCollum, Nina Simmonds, J. Ernestine Becker & R.W. Bunting, 'The effect of additions of fluorine to the diet of the rat on the quality of the teeth', *Journal of Biological Chemistry* 63, 1925, 553.
22. Medical Research Council Minutes, 22 May 1940, Council Papers 1941, MS-1636/001, University of Otago Medical Library: Historical Collection, Hocken Collections Uare Taoka o Hākena, University of Otago.
23. Bell, 'Report of nutritionist 1942–43'.
24. Undated interview, Transcript of interviews with Dr Bell, MS-1078/003, Dr Muriel Bell: Papers.
25. Muriel E. Bell, 'Report of Nutrition Committee for year ending 31 March 1948', Nutrition reports, MS-1078/071.
26. Marion Robinson, interview with Ruth Barton, 11–12 February 1994, OHA 2637, Oral History Collection, Alexander Turnbull Library, Wellington.
27. Ola Rudman, 'Seeing's believing', *New Zealand Women's Weekly,* 12 December 1946, 18.
28. Minutes, Nutrition Committee, 26 April 1945, Nutrition reports, MS-1078/071.
29. 'Report of the Nutrition Committee for the year 1948–49', Council Papers, MS-1636/011, University of Otago Medical Library: Historical Collection; Appraisal of Rex Malthus, Medical Research Council Finance 1947–51, H 1 240/1/4, Department of Health, National Archives, Wellington.
30. John Malcolm to T.R. Ritchie, 21 March 1949, Medical Research Nutrition Appointment of Members of Committee 1949–51, YCBN 5977 60i 260/2/8, National Archives, Auckland.
31. Bell, 'Report of Nutrition Committee for year ending 31 March 1948.'
32. Bell, *Nutrition in the First Five Years*, 40.
33. Minutes, Medical Research Council, 20 May 1948, Medical Research Council Minutes of meeting and agenda 1937–1950, H 1 240/1/7, Department of Health, National Archives, Wellington.
34. Muriel E. Bell to J.F. Tasker, secretary of the Medical Research Council, 20 June 1949, Medical Research Council Finance 1947–51, H 1 240/1/4.

CHAPTER EIGHT: AFFLUENCE AND FRAGMENTING PRIORITIES IN THE 1950s

1. Tom Jaine, 'Introduction', in Sir Jack C. Drummond, Anne Wilbraham and Dorothy F. Hollingsworth, *The Englishman's Food: Five centuries of English diet* (1957; repr., London: Pimlico, 1991), 10.
2. Dorothy Porter, 'Introduction', in *Social Medicine and Medical Sociology in the Twentieth Century,* ed. Dorothy Porter and Wellcome Institute for the History of Medicine (Amsterdam: Rodopi, 1997), 15.
3. Simon Szreter, *Health and Wealth: Studies in history and policy* (Rochester, NY: University of Rochester, 2007), 24.

4. Virginia Berridge, *Making Health Policy: Networks in research and policy after 1945* (Amsterdam: Rodopi, 2005), 12.
5. A.W. Beasley, 'Burns, Charles Ritchie, 1898–1985', Dictionary of New Zealand Biography: www.teara.govt.nz/en/biographies/5b50/burns-charles-ritchie
6. New Zealand Medical Research Council, 'Nutrition Research Committee', 1951, Dr Muriel Bell, AG-007-004/262, Royal New Zealand Plunket Society: Records, Hocken Collections Uare Taoka o Hākena, University of Otago.
7. Celia Petty, 'Primary research and public health: The prioritization of nutrition research in inter-war Britain', in *Historical Perspectives on the Role of the MRC*, ed. Joan Austoker and Linda Bryder (Oxford: Oxford University Press, 1989), 83–108.
8. T.R. Ritchie, acting director general of health, to Mabel Howard, minister of health, 8 July 1947, Medical Research Council Finance 1947–51, H 1 240/1/4, National Archives, Wellington.
9. 'Report: Nutrition Research Department of Medical Research Council New Zealand', c. 1961, Papers and booklets relating to the history of Nutrition Research Department of MRCNZ, MS-1078/107, Dr Muriel Bell: Papers, Hocken Collections Uare Taoka o Hākena, University of Otago.
10. Kenneth J. Carpenter, 'Nutritional diseases', in *Companion Encyclopedia of the History of Medicine*, vol. 1, ed. W.F. Bynum and Roy Porter (London: Routledge, 1993), 480.
11. Muriel E. Bell to M. Abraham, 8 November 1949, Nutrition General 1946–49, H 1 31, National Archives, Wellington.
12. 'International Survey of Programmes of Social Development', September 1953, Nutrition General 1950–53, H 1 31, National Archives, Wellington.
13. Lucy Wills and Muriel E. Bell, 'The serum-protein levels of Samoans, Fijians and Indians in Fiji', *Lancet 257*, no. 6659, 14 April 1951, 820.
14. 'Dr Muriel Bell returns after islands survey', *Evening Star,* 14 March 1950.
15. Muriel E. Bell and Lucy Wills, 'Racial differences in incidence of pre-eclampsia and eclampsia in Fiji', *Journal of Obstetrics and Gynaecology of the British Empire 62*, no. 6, December 1955, 917–21.
16. Ibid., 920.
17. 'Report: Nutrition Research Department of Medical Research Council of New Zealand'.
18. Muriel E. Bell, 'Report of nutritionist, 1950', Nutrition Research Committee papers, MS-1078/070, Dr Muriel Bell: Papers.
19. Muriel E. Bell to C.W. Morrison, dominion secretary, Council of Organisations for Relief Services Overseas, n.d., Medical Adviser Number 27 – correspondence to Dr Muriel Bell, AG-007-004/035, Royal New Zealand Plunket Society: Records.
20. Muriel E. Bell and Lucy Wills, 'Report on pilot survey on state of nutrition of Fijians and Indians in Fiji, January–February 1950', International Affairs South Pacific Commission Work Programme Nutrition and Diet, 1949–1950, EA

W2619 116/10/4/6 pt1, National Archives, Wellington.
21. 'Dr Muriel Bell returns'.
22. Muriel E. Bell, 'A nutrition officer's experiences visiting the southwest Pacific islands', *Nutrition Reviews* 14, no. 2, February 1956, 33–36.
23. Muriel E. Bell, 'Report of Nutritionist: Report on leave during 24 June 1952 to 16 March 1953', Nutrition reports, MS-1078/007, Dr Muriel Bell: Papers.
24. Minutes of Central Milk Council, 16–17 July 1953, Minutes Central Milk Council 1952–53, AATJ W4100 9 2, National Archives, Wellington.
25. R.A. Paterson to Muriel E. Bell, 26 May 1952, Overseas study tour by Dr Bell looking at milk treatment stations, MS-1078/088, Dr Muriel Bell: Papers.
26. Bell, 'Report of Nutritionist: Report on leave'.
27. Ibid.
28. Ibid.
29. Ibid.
30. Ibid.
31. Ibid.
32. 'Fatties Anon', *Evening Star,* 8 May 1953.
33. Undated interview, Transcript of interviews with Dr Bell, MS-1078/003, Dr Muriel Bell: Papers.
34. Muriel E. Bell, 'Report of Nutrition Research Committee for year ending 31 March 1953', Nutrition reports, MS-1078/007.
35. Bell, 'Report of Nutrition Research Committee for year ending 31 March 1953'.
36. Bell, 'Report of nutritionist: Report on leave'.
37. Klaus Schwarz to Muriel E. Bell, 1 April 1959, Klaus Schwarz correspondence and reprints of his articles, MS-1078/080, Dr Muriel Bell: Papers.
38. Muriel E. Bell, 'Mineral deficiencies in New Zealand', *Journal of the American Dental Association 40,* no. 3, 1962, 207.
39. Schwarz to Bell, 1 April 1959.
40. 'Those animal fats … How much is the car, not the cow, to blame?' *Otago Daily Times,* 29 January 1959.
41. Muriel E. Bell, 'Report: Nutrition Research Committee 1956–57', Correspondence, MS-1078/010, Dr Muriel Bell: Papers.
42. Muriel E. Bell to Endel Kask, 13 August 1957, Atherosclerosis papers, MS-1078/075, Dr Muriel Bell: Papers.
43. Muriel Livingstone, Muriel E. Bell, F.B. Shorland, T. Gerson and R.P. Hansen, 'The metabolism in the rat of naturally occurring (+)-14-methylhexadecanoic acid', *Biochemical Journal 65*, no. 3, 1957, 438–40.
44. 'Report of Nutrition Research Committee for year ending March 31st 1952', Nutrition reports, MS-1078/007.
45. Muriel E. Bell, 'Nutrition research: General speech', Dr Bell's radio talks and articles, MS-1078/058, Dr Muriel Bell: Papers.
46. Hugh M. Sinclair, 'Food and health', *British Medical Journal*, no. 2, 14 December 1957, 1424.

47. Muriel E. Bell, 'Home Science refresher course, January 1959: Animal fat in the diet', Notes and Articles on Nutrition, apparently collected by Dr Muriel Bell, University of Otago Medical Library: Historical Collection, MS-1682/007, Hocken Collections Uare Taoka o Hākena, University of Otago.
48. 'The cause of obesity said to be over-eating', *Otago Daily Times,* 26 January 1959.
49. Bell, 'Nutrition research: General speech'.
50. Muriel E. Bell, 'Some New Zealand research aspects of animal fats considered in relation to diet and cardiovascular disease', *New Zealand Dietetic Journal 11*, no. 2, 1957, 13.
51. Bell to Kask, 13 August 1957.
52. Charles Burns to Muriel E. Bell, 2 July 1958, Nutrition Research Committee papers, MS-1078/070.
53. Ibid.
54. Hilda Ross, minister of social welfare, to Ralph Hanan, minister of health, 21 October 1957, Medical Research Council Nutrition Research Committee annual reports and estimated expenditure 1951–1967, YCBN 5977 16a 245/15/3, National Archives, Auckland.
55. Muriel E. Bell to Sir Edmund Hillary, 14 September 1955, MS-Papers 1342–83, Sir E. Marsden Papers, Alexander Turnbull Library, Wellington.
56. Muriel E. Bell, 'Rations for the New Zealand trans-Antarctic expedition', *New Zealand Medical Journal 61*, no. 312, 1957, 289–304.
57. A.S. Helm, secretary, Ross Sea Committee, to Muriel E. Bell, 3 February 1958, Nutrition Research Committee papers, MS-1078/070.
58. 'Antarctic expedition food has ample calorie value', *Otago Daily Times,* 23 January 1957.
59. Transcript of interview with Dr Muriel Bell, 'Food and good health', 1961, Biographical information on Dr Bell and notes relating to nutrition, MS-1078/108, Dr Muriel Bell: Papers.
60. Doctor Muriel Bell, ID 26100, Ngā Taonga Sound and Vision, Christchurch.

CHAPTER NINE: 'BATTLE-AXE BELL'

1. Minutes of Nutrition Research Committee, 7 February 1964, Nutrition Research Committee papers, MS-1078/070, Dr Muriel Bell: Papers, Hocken Collections Uare Taoka o Hākena, University of Otago.
2. Undated interview, Nutrition research reports and notes, MS-1078/100, Dr Muriel Bell: Papers.
3. J.R. Robinson, 'Obituary: Muriel Emma Bell', *New Zealand Medical Journal 79*, no. 518, June 1974, 1083.
4. Michael Belgrave, 'Needs and the state: Evolving social policy in New Zealand history', in *Past Judgement: Social policy in New Zealand history,* ed. Bronwyn Dalley and Margaret Tennant (Dunedin: University of Otago Press, 2004), 35.
5. Oliver Duff, *Ourselves Today* (Christchurch: Pegasus Press, 1959), 25–26.

6. Muriel E. Bell, 'Report: Nutrition Research Committee 1956–1957', Correspondence, MS-1078/010, Dr Muriel Bell: Papers.
7. Muriel E. Bell, 'No. 196: Fluorine and teeth'; 'No. 197: Fluorine and teeth (II)'; 'No. 198: Fluorine and teeth (III)', Correspondence and clippings relating to Dr Bell's New Zealand *Listener* articles, MS-1078/063, Dr Muriel Bell: Papers.
8. 'Dr Muriel Bell', *New Zealand Dental Journal 60*, October 1964, 333.
9. Quoted in C.N. Derek Taylor, 'Fluoridation comes to Hastings', *New Zealand Medical Journal 54*, no. 299, February 1955, 23.
10. Muriel E. Bell, 'Mineral deficiencies in New Zealand', *Journal of the American Dental Association 40*, no. 3, March 1962, 205.
11. Advertisement, 1959, Fluoridation clippings and related papers, MS-1078/072, Dr Muriel Bell: Papers.
12. C.N. Derek Taylor, 'Health education aspects of fluoridation in New Zealand', *New Zealand Medical Journal 56*, 1957, 321–25.
13. Taylor, 'Fluoridation comes to Hastings', 23.
14. Taylor, 'Health education aspects of fluoridation in New Zealand'.
15. Jim Hefford, interview with author, 13 May 2005.
16. Ibid.
17. Alfred Hefford to Cicely Marks, 28 January 1955, Jim Hefford, private collection.
18. Alfred Hefford to Cicely Marks, 21 November 1953, Jim Hefford, private collection.
19. Alfred Hefford to Cicely Marks, 21 July 1954, Jim Hefford, private collection.
20. Alfred Hefford to Cicely Marks, 9 November 1954, Jim Hefford, private collection.
21. Alfred Hefford to Cicely Marks, 31 December 1956, Jim Hefford, private collection.
22. 'Dr Muriel Bell', The best women I have known, MS-Papers-5433-26, Ruth Wilson: Personal papers, Alexander Turnbull Library, Wellington.
23. Muriel E. Bell, 'Report: Nutrition Research Committee 1956–1957', Correspondence, MS-1078/010.
24. R.S. Malthus, 'Report for 1956–57', Nutrition Research Committee, 31 March 1957, Nutrition Research Committee papers, MS-1078/070.
25. New Zealand Commission of Inquiry on the Fluoridation of Public Water Supplies, *Report of the Commission of Inquiry on the Fluoridation of Public Water Supplies* (Wellington: R.E. Owen, Government Printer, 1957), 119.
26. Minutes of Nutrition Research Committee, 31 March 1957, Nutrition Research Committee papers, MS-1078/070.
27. New Zealand Commission of Inquiry, *Report of the Commission of Inquiry*, 58.
28. 'Commission of inquiry to investigate fluoridation: Evidence of Muriel Emma Bell', Fluoridation clippings and related papers, MS-1078/072.
29. Ibid.
30. Muriel E. Bell, 'Supplementary statement made at the Dunedin session of the commission of inquiry into the fluoridation of water', Fluoridation clippings and related papers, MS-1078/072.

31. 'Dr Muriel Bell, advocate of fluoridation', *Otago Daily Times*, 30 November 1956.
32. 'Commission of inquiry to investigate fluoridation: Evidence of Muriel Emma Bell'.
33. New Zealand Commission of Inquiry, *Report of the Commission of Inquiry*, 131, 75–76.
34. Kaj Roholm, *Fluorine Intoxication: A clinical-hygienic study with a review of the literature and some experimental investigations* (London: H.K. Lewis and Co., 1937).
35. Mira Louise, *Fluoridation the Poisoner* (Adelaide: Shipping Newspaper (SA) Ltd, 1954).
36. Alfred Hefford to Cicely Marks, 25 February 1954, Jim Hefford, private collection.
37. New Zealand Commission of Inquiry, *Report of the Commission of Inquiry*, 97.
38. Muriel E. Bell to Michael Watt, 3 November 1943, Medical Research Nutrition Research, H 1 240/2, National Archives, Wellington.
39. New Zealand Commission of Inquiry, *Report of the Commission of Inquiry*, 6–7.
40. Ibid., 15.
41. *Southland Times*, 28 November 1959, Fluoridation clippings and related papers, MS-1078/072.
42. Austin Mitchell, 'Fluoridation in Dunedin: A study of pressure groups and public opinion', *Political Science 12*, no. 1, March 1960, 73.
43. Taylor, 'Fluoridation comes to Hastings', 23.
44. Muriel E. Bell, letter to the editor, *Evening Star*, 7 November 1959.
45. Mitchell, 'Fluoridation in Dunedin', 72.
46. Marion Robinson, interview with Ruth Barton, Dunedin, 11–12 February 1994, OHA 2637, Alexander Turnbull Library, Wellington.
47. D.M. Robinson to H.G.R. Mason, minister of health, 20 August 1958, H 1 31 Nutrition General 1958–61, National Archives, Wellington.
48. Mitchell, 'Fluoridation in Dunedin', 81.
49. T.W.H. Brooking, *A History of Dentistry in New Zealand* (Dunedin: New Zealand Dental Association, 1980), 184.
50. P.J. Scott, 'Nutrition, science and social responsibility', *Proceedings of the Nutrition Society of New Zealand 8*, 1983, 6.
51. Letter from Muriel E. Bell to Col. J. Ferris Fuller, director of dental services, (army, air, navy), 20 May 1958, Fluoridation, MS-Papers-6167-09, Fuller, James Ferris (Brigadier) 1913–2001: Papers, Alexander Turnbull Library, Wellington.
52. Mitchell, 'Fluoridation in Dunedin', 75.
53. Otago Children's Dental Health Association, *The Reason Why*? (Wellington: R.E. Owen, Government Printer, 1959).
54. T.G. Ludwig, 'The Hastings fluoridation project: Dental effects between 1954 and 1957', interim report, 4; subsequently published in *New Zealand Dental Journal 65*, 1961, 175–79.
55. Mitchell, 'Fluoridation in Dunedin', 76.

56. *Evening Star,* 23 November 1959.
57. 'The reason why', *Otago Daily Times*, 23 November 1959.
58. Muriel E. Bell to J. Ferris Fuller, 29 May 1958, Fluoridation, MS-Papers-6167-09.
59. Barbara Smith, interview with author, 12 April 2005.
60. Minutes of Board of Health, 25 November 1959, Board of Health Meeting Minutes 1953–61, H 1 29/2/2, National Archives, Wellington.
61. Mitchell, 'Fluoridation in Dunedin', 92–93.
62. *Evening Star*, 23 November 1959.
63. *Southland Times,* 28 November 1959.
64. 'Report: Nutrition Research Department of the Medical Research Council of New Zealand', c. 1961, Papers and booklets relating to the history of Nutrition Research Department of MRCNZ, MS-1078/107, Dr Muriel Bell: Papers.
65. Charles R. Burns to Muriel E. Bell, 17 January 1963, Dr Charles Burns correspondence, MS-1078/091, Dr Muriel Bell: Papers.
66. H.B. Turbott, 'A letter to mothers re: fluoride tablets for better dental health', n.d., cited in Derek Dow, *Safeguarding the Public Health: A history of the New Zealand Department of Health* (Wellington: Victoria University Press, 1995), 191.
67. 'Report: Nutrition Research Department of the Medical Research Council of New Zealand'.
68. Bell, 'Mineral deficiencies in New Zealand', 205.
69. Ibid.
70. Muriel E. Bell, 'Reassuring evidence of fluorine homeostasis', *New Zealand Medical Journal* 63, no. 378, February 1964, 68.
71. Ibid.
72. Dow, *Safeguarding the Public Health*, 172.
73. Muriel E. Bell to J.C. Lucas, town clerk, Dunedin City Corporation, 2 February 1966, Rex Malthus, personal collection.
74. Undated interview, Nutrition research reports and notes, MS-1078/100.

CHAPTER TEN: THE FINAL STRUGGLE

1. Newspaper clipping (including a photo of Muriel on her return to Dunedin in the regalia of FRACP), Nutrition research reports and notes, MS-1078/100, Dr Muriel Bell: Papers, Hocken Collections Uare Taoka o Hākena, University of Otago.
2. Joan Harris, New Zealand executive secretary, Otago University Association Home Science Alumnae, to Leonard Wright, mayor of Dunedin, 11 November 1958, Home Science Alumnae MS-1078/18, Dr Muriel Bell: Papers.
3. Ibid.
4. Charles R. Burns, 'Review of *Normal Nutrition*', *New Zealand Medical Journal* 59, August 1960, 405.
5. J.F. Copplestone, 'Public health or the health of the public?' *Public Health* 79, no. 3, 1964, 29.

6. J.H. Thomas, chair, Education Board of the District of South Auckland, 'South Auckland Education Board: Submission on School Milk Scheme', September 1960, Milk in Schools, MS-1078/001, Dr Muriel Bell: Papers.
7. 'Milk at school held necessary', *Otago Daily Times*, n.d., Biographical information on Dr Bell and notes relating to nutrition, MS-1078/108, Dr Muriel Bell: Papers.
8. 'Napier doctors' broadside', *New Zealand Medical Journal 58* (October 1959), Biographical information on Dr Bell and notes relating to nutrition, MS-1078/108.
9. '"Too much milk" attack "illogical" says nutritionist', *Dominion*, 2 November 1957; 'Dr Bell defends milk as food', *Otago Daily Times,* 5 November 1957.
10. Muriel E. Bell, 'Growth rates of children and adolescents in New Zealand and in Britain', *Journal of the Association of Home Science Alumnae (NZ) 30*, July 1961, 4.
11. Muriel E. Bell, 'Osteoporosis as a dietary problem', *Journal of the New Zealand Dietetic Association 15*, no. 1, June 1961, 6.
12. 'Milk in schools: "Much unfounded talk about waste"', *Otago Daily Times*, 24 June 1955.
13. 'Milk at school held necessary'.
14. Muriel E. Bell, handwritten notes on overseas tour 1963, n.d., Nutritional fats, and cholesterol, notes and conference address, MS-1078/060, Dr Muriel Bell: Papers.
15. 'Milk in schools scheme must not be wrecked', *New Zealand Parent and Child 9*, no. 1, March–April 1961, 31.
16. 'Some opinions on school milk', *National Education 42*, December 1960, 506–07.
17. Undated interview, Nutrition research reports and notes, MS-1078/100.
18. 'Nutrition research to continue in city', *Otago Daily Times*, 11 July 1962.
19. 'Nutrition Research Committee report for 1960', n.d., Nutrition Research Committee papers, MS-1078/070.
20. H.G.R. Mason, minister of health, to cabinet, 25 July 1960, Nutrition Joint FAO WHO Expert Commission on Nutrition 1951–64, H 1 2045 31/7, National Archives, Wellington.
21. Bell, 'Growth rates of children and adolescents'.
22. Muriel E. Bell, 'Calories, corpulence, cholesterol, coronaries, cows, corn, cars, et cetera', *Public Health: Journal of the New Zealand Branch of the Royal Society for the Promotion of Health 76,* no. 3, 1961, 16.
23. 'Nutrition Research Committee report for 1960'. 'Nutrition research to continue in city'.
24. Muriel E. Bell, handwritten notes, undated, Nutritional fats, and cholesterol, notes and conference address, MS-1078/060.
25. 'Nutrition Research Committee report', n.d. [c. 1958], Nutrition Research Committee papers, MS-1078/070.
26. Ruth Wilson, 'Dr Muriel Bell: The best women I have known', MS-

Papers-5433-26, Ruth Wilson: Personal papers, Alexander Turnbull Library, Wellington.

27. Charles R. Burns to Muriel E. Bell, 18 April 1963, Dr Charles Burns Correspondence, MS-1078/091, Dr Muriel Bell: Papers.
28. Minutes of special meeting of Nutrition Research Committee, 10 April 1963, Nutrition Research Committee papers, MS-1078/070.
29. Ibid.
30. Transcript of interview with Dr Muriel Bell, 'Food and good health', 1961, Biographical information on Dr Bell and notes relating to nutrition, MS-1078/108.
31. 'Future of nutrition research and nutrition services, March 1962', Nutrition Research Committee papers, MS-1078/070.
32. Ibid.
33. Charles R. Burns to Muriel E. Bell, 8 December 1962, Dr Charles Burns Correspondence, MS-1078/091.
34. Minutes of Nutrition Research Committee, 14 April 1962, Nutrition Research Committee Papers, MS-1078/070.
35. Burns to Bell, 8 December 1962.
36. Burns to Bell, 18 April 1963.
37. Prime minister Keith Holyoake to Muriel E. Bell, 30 April 1963, Medical Research Council Nutrition Research Committee staff 1951–66, YVBN 5977 16b 145/12/2, National Archives, Auckland.
38. Howard P. Himsworth, 'Report to the New Zealand Medical Research Council on the present position and organisation for medical research in New Zealand', 4 June 1963, Board of Health Minutes 1961–67, H 1 2148 29/2/2, National Archives, Wellington.
39. F.B. Shorland, 'Vote of thanks', in Charles R. Burns, *Some Aspects of Alcohol Use and Human Nutrition, with Special Reference to the Acute Alcohol Withdrawal Syndrome: Third Muriel Bell Memorial Lecture*, 10 February 1977 (Palmerston North: Nutrition Society of New Zealand, 1977), 27.
40. Marion Robinson, interview with Ruth Barton, Dunedin, 11–12 February 1994, OHA 2637, Alexander Turnbull Library, Wellington.
41. Derek A. Dow, 'Turbott, Harold Bertram, 1899–1988', Dictionary of New Zealand Biography: www.teara.govt.nz/en/biographies/5t21/turbott-harold-bertram
42. 'Editorial: Shock for research', *Otago Daily Times*, 16 August 1963.
43. Muriel E. Bell, 'Report on overseas tour May 23rd to Sept 2nd 1961', Dr Bell's radio talks and articles, MS-1078/058, Dr Muriel Bell: Papers.
44. Burns, *Some Aspects of Alcohol Use and Human Nutrition*, 3.
45. 'Plunket protest at disbanding of nutrition unit', *Clutha Leader*, 11 September 1963.
46. National Council of Women to Arnold Nordmeyer, minister of health, 22 November 1944, Miscellaneous medical research nutrition 1944–45, H 1 172/240/2, National Archives, Wellington.

47. Minutes of Consumer Council, 9 October 1963, Consumer Council meetings minutes 1959–64, AAFB 632 W2788 127 377/26/1, National Archives, Wellington.
48. Patricia Coleman, Proposed questions for Mrs McMillan, MP for Dunedin North, for parliament, Dr Muriel Bell, MS-1516/18, Home Science Alumnae, Hocken Collections Uare Taoka o Hākena, University of Otago.
49. F.B. Shorland, Meeting of Nutrition Research Committee, 6 September 1963, Dr Bell's radio talks and articles, MS-1078/058.
50. Ibid.
51. Margaret W. Rossiter, 'The men move in: Home economics, 1950–1970', in *Rethinking Home Economics*, ed. Sarah Stage and Virginia B. Vincenti (Ithaca, NY: Cornell University Press, 1997), 96–117.
52. Shorland, 'Vote of thanks'.
53. E.G. Sayers, dean, Otago Medical School, to unknown recipient, 19 December 1963, Medical Research Council Nutrition Research Committee annual reports and estimated expenditure 1951–1967, YCBN 5977 16a 245/15/3, National Archives, Auckland.
54. Minutes of Nutrition Research Committee, 7 February 1964, Nutrition Research Committee papers, MS-1078/070.
55. 'Luncheon to honour Dr Bell', *Journal of the Association of Home Science Alumnae (NZ) 33*, 1964, 42.
56. 'Citation by Professor Horsman, public orator, University of Otago, at Dunedin Town Hall, on occasion of graduation ceremony, December 5, 1968, at which Honorary Doctorate of Science was conferred on Dr Muriel E. Bell', Robin McLaughlin, personal collection.
57. Shorland, 'Vote of thanks'.
58. Philippa Mein Smith, 'Bell, Muriel Emma, 1989–1974', Dictionary of New Zealand Biography: www.teara.govt.nz/en/biographies/4b21/bell-muriel-emma
59. Muriel E. Bell, 'Toxicology of karaka kernel, karakin and β-nitropropionic acid', *New Zealand Journal of Science 13*, 1974, 327–34.
60. Jean Caradus Williams, interview with author, April 2005.
61. Mona Randall, interview with author, August 2005.

INDEX